THE MINI ROUGH GUIDE TO
ZÁKYNTHOS

ROUGH GUIDES

YOUR TAILOR-MADE TRIP
STARTS HERE

Tailor-made trips and unique adventures crafted by local experts

Rough Guides has been inspiring travellers for more than 35 years. Leave it to our local experts to create your perfect itinerary and book it at local rates.

Don't follow the crowd – find your own path.

HOW ROUGHGUIDES.COM/TRIPS WORKS

STEP 1 Pick your dream destination, tell us what you want and submit an enquiry.

STEP 2 Fill in a short form to tell your local expert about your dream trip and preferences.

STEP 3 Our local expert will craft your tailor-made itinerary. You'll be able to tweak and refine it until you're completely satisfied.

STEP 4 Book online with ease, pack your bags and enjoy the trip! Our local expert will be on hand 24/7 while you're on the road.

PLAN AND BOOK YOUR TRIP AT
ROUGHGUIDES.COM/TRIPS

HOW TO DOWNLOAD YOUR FREE EBOOK

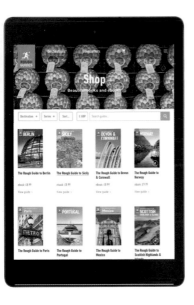

1. Visit **www.roughguides.com/free-ebook** or scan the **QR code** below

2. Enter the code **zakynthos349**

3. Follow the simple step-by-step instructions

For troubleshooting contact: mail@roughguides.com

10 THINGS NOT TO MISS

A PERFECT TOUR

Day 1

Zákynthos Town. In the morning, visit the Zákynthos and Solomos museums and soak up the atmosphere of central Platía Solomoú, before having a light lunch at nearby *Varkarola*. After a siesta, stroll along the seafront for a coffee or cocktail and enjoy a fish dinner at *Komis* after viewing the impressive interior of Ágios Dhionýsios cathedral.

Day 2

Boat tour of the island. Choose from one of the many daily boat tours that circumnavigate the island, usually in an anti-clockwise direction. This is the best way to admire the stunning coastline of Zákynthos: the two main highlights are the Blue Caves and Shipwreck Bay, but look out for the Kerí caves too. In the evening, dine at *Malanos* taverna.

Day 3

Vasilikós Peninsula and Laganás Bay. Rent a car for the rest of the week and start with a gentle drive down the Vasilikós Peninsula, stopping to visit the Sea Turtle Rescue and Information Centre at Yérakas. Don't forget to swim at the splendid beach here! After lunch at *To Triodi* in Yérakas, head out for another dip at Límni Kerioú at the far end of Laganás Bay, before some much-needed bar action in central Laganás.

Day 4

Rugged Zákynthos. Pack your bags and take a drive across the fertile plain to the rugged western mountains, visiting traditional villages and monasteries, including the weaving and embroidery centre of Volímes. Take a dip at the delightful little beach of Xyngiá, before driving towards the island's northern tip at Cape Skinári to stay at the unique Anemomilos converted windmills before eating supper at the affiliated taverna.

Day 5

Sweeping views and sea caves in the north of the island. Enjoy the stunning scenery of Alykés Bay and over to Kefaloniá from just outside of Katastári (the largest village outside the capital) along the road that continues over to the west coast. Stop off at the beach at Makrýs Yialós. and swim into one of the many sea caves before enjoying lunch at a local seaside taverna. If any of those tavernas don't take your fancy, further on is the tiny headland of Mikrónisi, where you can eat at the single taverna overlooking boats bobbing in the small inlet. The boats are available to rent if you fancy a sea-based tour of the area.

Day 6

Boat trip to Blue Caves and Shipwreck Bay. If you didn't take a full round-the-island trip on Day 2, the little port of Ágios Nikólaos is the starting point for a shorter jaunt to the nearby Blue Caves, and onward to Shipwreck Bay, weather permitting!

Day 7

Onward. From the Cape Skinári region you are perfectly placed to board the regular morning ferry from Ágios Nikólaos to Pesádha on Kefaloniá, should that island figure next on your travel plans.

CONTENTS

HIGHLIGHTS

A NOTE TO READERS

At Rough Guides, we always strive to bring you the most up-to-date information. This book was produced during a period of continuing uncertainty caused by the Covid-19 pandemic, so please note that content is more subject to change than usual. We recommend checking the latest restrictions and official guidance.

OVERVIEW

Zákynthos (commonly also known as 'Zante') is the southeast-ernmost and third largest of the six principal Ionian islands in the sea of the same name; remote Kýthira was historically a seventh Ionian island, but today is governed from Piraeus. Zákynthos is found off Greece's western coast, lying just off the western tip of the Peloponnese peninsula. The island's much-used alias, Zante, springs from the medieval ditty that went 'Zante, Zante, Fior di Levante', meaning 'Zante, Zante, flower of the East'; this was chanted because the island was so fragrant that passing sailors could sense its presence from the blossom scents that wafted out to sea long before they could actually see it.

Like nearby Kefaloniá, Zákynthos is predominantly made up of heavily folded Cretaceous limestones. Geologically speaking, the two islands form a unit, separated from Corfu to the north by the Kefaloniá fault zone. On Zákynthos in particular the island's topography is easily related to its underlying geology; the western mountains (the highest point being the 756-metre Vrahiónas) are made of relatively hard Cretaceous limestones, while the gentler east is largely made up of Plio-Pleistocene mudstone or sandstone deposits. The Vasilikós Peninsula is a combination of hard Triassic evaporites and Plio-Pleistocene marls. Markedly folded rock strata point to a turbulent geological history, and both islands' location along the Hellenic Subduction Zone (where the African tectonic plate is burrowing beneath the Aegean plate) gives rise to frequent earthquakes.

The area of Zákynthos extends to just under 406 sq km (just less than 157 sq miles) and is home to just fewer than 40,000 year-round residents (reduced from almost 50,000 in 1906). Although definitive figures from Greece's 2021 census are not yet available,

Ruins of the monastery of Panagia Skopiotissa

preliminary results suggest that no local population growth will be registered.

In antiquity, Homer related that Zakynthos was the son of King Dardanos of the Peloponnese. Zakynthos settled on the island – thereby lending it his name – and created the fortification of Psophis, named after the ancient town in Arkadia from which he came. It is possible that the location of Psophis was on the site of the present-day *kástro* at Bóhali (see page 36).

The island of Zákynthos was an Athenian ally during the Peloponnesian Wars (431–404 BC); Athenian fleets made good use of the pitch near the lake of Kerí to make necessary repairs to their ships. Sadly, most (though not all) of these pitch wells have long since dried up.

After a somewhat lacklustre period under Roman and then Byzantine rule, Zákynthos was – like all of the other Ionian islands – seized by the Venetian Republic in 1386 or shortly thereafter, and remained a Venetian overseas possession until 1797 when Napoleon Bonaparte dissolved the Venetian empire. These years of Venetian tenure have left a visible mark on Zakynthian cuisine, crops, music, architecture and social mores which endures even to the present day.

The brief interlude of the semi-autonomous Septinsular Republic from 1799 until 1807, and another French interlude until 1815, was succeeded by a British protectorate which lasted until Zákynthos, along with the other Ionian Islands, was ceded to Greece in 1864 as a condition of Prince William of Denmark ascending the Greek throne as King George I.

During World War I, Zákynthos was – like much of Greece – divided into republican (that is to say, pro-Eleftherios Venizelos, a prominent leader of the Greek national liberation movement) and royalist factions. The balance was tipped towards the former by the French, who got involved in the conflicts in 1915 and again in 1917.

Today the island is still fertile, heavily vegetated with Mediterranean scrub and wildflowers (though not much forest) and receives, like all of western Greece, considerable rainfall between October and April. Summer visitors, though, can count on reliably sunny days, with average air temperatures between 24°C and 27°C, reaching highs of almost 33° C during July and August. Sea temperatures can approach 27° C in August, while the water is comfortably swimmable from May until October.

Prominent Poets

Prominent Zakynthians include the poets Ugo Foscolo, Andreas Calvos and Dionysios Solomos; the lawyer and diplomat Dionysios Romas; and the World War II resistance heroes Loukas Karrer and Archbishop Chrysostomos.

TOURISM

The first package tourists arrived in 1982, brought by the British company Sunmed and later Club 18–30. Nowadays, scheduled airlines like easyJet and BA (May–Sept) serve the island direct from the UK, not just package charters. All of this has led to indiscriminate development along the south and east coast beaches of Zákynthos, bringing in its wake a huge annual influx of mostly British package tourists, although numbers have steeply declined in recent years due first to Greece's economic crisis and then to the Covid-19 pandemic.

Nevertheless, the boom years injected a considerable amount of cash into the local economy, although much of it remained in the hands of the major international tour operators and large hotel owners. The tourists have also brought with them some unwelcome social behaviour, including bouts of heavy drinking and occasional violence.

As well as this social disruption, there has been a huge environmental impact resulting from such a large number of visitors. Prior to the tourist boom the island was extremely poor, with a severely underdeveloped infrastructure. Eager to exploit a steady source of income, locals threw up shoddy hotels and resorts with little regard for their environmental impact,

Xigia Beach

never mind the water and sanitation needs of up to 700,000 visitors per year (although more recently, overseas arrivals are down to about a quarter of a million annually). By the mid-1990s it was realised that action needed to be taken to protect the endangered species that make their homes here, such as the loggerhead turtle, and to preserve sensitive areas. After a long – and occasionally bitter – campaign by Greek conservationist activists, the National Marine Park of Zákynthos was established in 1999 (see page 45). Over two decades later, there is still friction between ecologists and local businessmen, because many of the protective measures stipulated by law have not been fully implemented in practice.

WILDLIFE ON ZAKYNTHOS

As well as being home to several species of mammal, Zákynthos has a number of interesting reptiles. One of the most spectacular is the large but harmless-to-humans Aesculapian rat snake (*Zamenis longissimus*), which can grow up to 2m (6.5ft) in length; similarly gigantic are Montpelier snakes (*Malpolon monspessulanus*), again non-venomous rodent- and lizard-catchers. Small birds include woodchat shrikes (*Lanius senator*) and beautiful golden orioles (*Oriolus oriolus*). In scrubland or agricultural areas, three kinds of warblers may be found. Among birds of prey, you may sight Eleonora's falcons swooping about the cliffs of the north and west coasts, and adorable little owls (*Athena noctua*), which are often visible and audible by day – they perch on utility wires and ruined buildings. Listen out by night for the tiny Scops owl (*Otus scops*), much more often heard than seen (its distinctive, repetitive pewping sounds like a submarine's sonar), and barn owls (*Tito alba*). The headline wildlife species of Zákynthos is, however, the majestic loggerhead sea turtle; see page 46 .

HISTORY AND CULTURE

Evidence of early human settlement on the southern Ionian Islands is scarce. There has been little excavation of specifically Palaeolithic and Neolithic sites, though a number of artefacts, such as flint hand tools like scrapers have been found. The earliest human presence is thought to date from the mid-Palaeolithic era (*c.*50,000 years ago), when, due to Ice Age reduction in sea levels, the Ionians were joined to present-day Greece and Italy. It is thought that groups of hunters arrived in the region, probably from the Píndhos mountains (northern Greece) and the Peloponnese. Some of them settled on the island of Zákynthos.

THE BRONZE AGE

Archeologists know that there was a thriving Bronze Age society on neighbouring Kefaloniá island. As yet, aside from some Bronze-Age tombs close to Kambí in the far west, there is little corresponding evidence from Zákynthos.

ODYSSEUS

Homeric epic *The Odyssey* follows the adventures of its eponymous hero from Troy, on the northwest coast of Anatolia, back home to mythical Ithaca. For a long time it was assumed that ancient Ithaca was present-day Itháki and numerous local features were named after events in the epic. However, there is scant archeological evidence to back these claims and the latest thinking points to southern Kefaloniá as the most likely spot for the kingdom. Zákynthos is completely out of the running, although it is mentioned by name in both *The Odyssey* and *The Iliad*.

THE ARCHAIC, CLASSICAL AND HELLENISTIC PERIODS

The origins of the earliest rulers of Zákynthos are the subjects of Greek mythology. However, there are more recent historical references that shed some light; Zákynthos was mentioned by both Herodotus and Thucydides. Zákynthos seems to have been for some centuries independent, ruled by leaders who originally came from the Peloponnese. This independence lasted for a fairly long time until just before the outbreak of the Peloponnesian War (431 BC), when the island was conquered by the Athenian general Tolmides; it was henceforth an Athenian ally during most of the conflict.

Towards the end (404 BC) of the Peloponnesian War, Zákynthos switched allegiance to Sparta. Much later, Philip V of Macedonia (ruled 221–179 BC) occupied Zákynthos – and temporarily lost the island to the Romans during the 2nd Punic War (218–202 BC). The definitive end of Hellenistic influence came when the Romans, under General Marcus Fulvius Nobilior, seized Zákynthos in 191 BC.

Mycenaean tomb

ROMANS, BYZANTINES AND FRANKS

From the Roman conquest to the advent of Byzantine rule in 337 AD, little of note is recorded in the history of Zákynthos. Zákynthos endured a sacking of the island by the Vandals in 474, the first of a number of attacks by outside forces.

As Byzantine imperial power waned, attacks on all of the Ionian Islands became more common, in particular by the Franks (a disparate group of largely Norman and Italian nobility). In 1204, after the sacking of Constantinople during the infamous Fourth Crusade, Zákynthos came under Frankish rule by the Tocco clan installed on Kefaloniá, which lasted uninterruptedly until 1479.

OTTOMANS AND VENETIANS

With the growing power of the Ottoman Empire to the east and northast, it was inevitable that the islands would soon receive their attention, and, in November 1479, Zákynthos and Kefaloniá were both attacked by the warlord Gedik Ahmad Pasha. The Ottomans overran both islands, taking many prisoners.

The Venetians were not deterred from their ideas of Mediterranean domination, however, and in 1484 regained control of Zákynthos by treaty, followed soon by neighbouring Kefaloniá (besieged successfully in December 1500). Thus, apart from a brief period, Zákynthos and the other Ionian islands (except for Lefkádha) are among the few areas of Greece not to have come under prolonged Ottoman rule or been noticeably influenced by it.

The neighbouring islands remained under Venetians suzerainty until 1797. This was a period of relative calm, although the Venetians ensured that both Zákynthos and Kefaloniá were heavily defended; the impressive castle at Bóhali above Zákynthos Town is a legacy of Venetian rule. Not only were the islands valued as staging posts for the Venetian navy, they were also prized for their agricultural production and the oldest among the numerous olive trees now seen on all of the Ionian islands were planted during this time.

One of the most visible legacies of the Venetian occupation is the large number of splendid churches, many with ornate, gilded

Earthquake zone

'The reason they build their houses so lowe [on Zákynthos] is because of the manifold Earthquakes which doe as much share this lland as any other place in the World.'
Thomas Coryat, 1612

baroque interiors, found on all Ionian islands. Much of the churches' interior decoration, and many of their icons, are the work of Cretan sculptors and painters, who fled to Zákynthos after the last Venetian stronghold on Crete fell to the Ottomans in 1669. Once arrived on the Ionian islands, they came under the influence of the Italian Renaissance, and the resulting artistic synthesis is known as painting of the Ionian School.

Foreign visitors during this period were often less than complimentary about the Zantiots. In 1632, the Scot Willie Lithgow wrote of them, 'The islanders are Greeks, a kind of subtile people, and great dissemblers.' Much later (1817), 18th-and-19th-century traveller and antiquarian Richard Chandler said that 'the inhabitants are chiefly Greeks … They are divided by internal feuds, and are exceedingly addicted to revenge, perpetrating assassinations even in their churches. The Moréa (Peloponnese) serves them as it were as a sanctuary, and abounds in fugitives for murder and misdemeanours.'

Local rulers came from aristocratic Venetian families, who acquired large estates after settling on the Ionian islands. Their names were inscribed in the so-called *Libro d'Oro* (Golden Book) on each island, the highest of the three social classes; the others were a nascent bourgeoisie – with limited political rights – and the popolari or oppressed peasantry, with none. The Greek Orthodox Church also assumed an inferior position to the Catholic, though the Venetians avidly intermarried with local women, who were not forced to convert to Catholicism.

The Assos Castle

With greater exposure to Western Europe, a number of schools were established, bringing currents of the Enlightenment to Zákynthos and the other Ionian islands. The language of the upper classes and of literature was Italian, or dialects thereof; the Greeks are very keen on nationalist Zakynthian poet Dionysios Solomos (1798–1857; see page 32), who first wrote in Italian, but later in Greek, while his fellow islander Ugo Foscolo (1787–1827), of mixed Venetian and Zakynthian Greek parentage, wrote exclusively in Italian during his regrettably short career which ended in the UK (he was initially buried in the Chiswick parish churchyard, close to The Mall and Hammersmith Pier, before his remains were transferred to Firenze's Santa Croce church in 1871). The London 'tomb' is now a cenotaph). Despite marginally improved living conditions, the Ionian islanders were not immune from the rumblings of nationalist discontent that grew steadily louder through the 18th century.

THE SEPTINSULAR REPUBLIC AND THE BRITISH

Discontent became more evident when, in July 1797, the islands were occupied by the Napoleonic French, who were obsessed by the archipelago as a strategic naval base. By decree, Bonaparte abolished all Venetian feudal privileges – on the main islands the local *Libro d'Oro* was burnt in public squares – and introduced radical proposals such as the abolition of organised religion. This proved unpopular with the locals, while rival powers, specifically the Orthodox Russians, were unhappy about Napoleon's widening sphere of influence, and agitation against the French began to brew. In October 1798 a joint Russian-Ottoman fleet sailed for these islands and, with local support, they fell easily to the invaders, who restored the privileges of the old nobility. They were the chief figures of the semi-autonomous republic established by an 1800 treaty in Constantinople.

This, the Eptánisos Politía (Septinsular Republic), became the first, nominally, independent modern Greek state. The fledgling state came to an end in 1807, when the Ionians reverted to the French under the Treaty of Tilsit, and in turn Zákynthos was occupied by the British during 1809, followed by all the other islands up to 1814. The British occupation, which lasted until 1864, was not an entirely happy time for

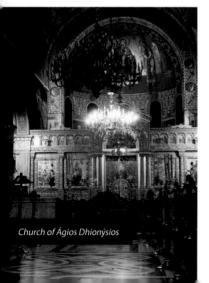

Church of Ágios Dhionýsios

the islanders. The first Lord High Commissioner, Thomas Maitland, was not at all well-liked by the islanders on account of his rudeness, aversion to personal hygiene and interference with Ionian assistance during the 1820s to the Greek insurrectionists on the mainland. Although the British did carry out a number of still-used public works on the larger islands, the local population became increasingly unhappy about foreign occupation and rule, especially after the creation of the neighbouring modern Greek state in 1828–31.

Although the largely complicit urban middle class had a comfortable standard of living, the peasant farmers were as downtrodden and poor as they had been under Venetian domination. Especially during 1851–52, the local island press agitated ceaselessly against British rule.

UNION WITH GREECE; WORLD WAR I

The Ionian islands had long been a place of refuge for independence fighters from the mainland (important military leader Kolokotronis landed on Zákynthos in 1805), and in 1864 the islanders' irredentist ambitions were finally realised when the British ceded the Ionian islands to Greece, as a condition for Danish Prince George of the Glucksberg dynasty ascending the Greek throne at King George I.

Union with Greece has never been universally popular in this archipelago, and there has long been a semi-serious secessionist movement afoot. The union yoked the most westernised portion of the Greek world to a struggling kingdom to the east. Local politics have often been at odds with the mainland; in recent decades left-of-centre political parties have enjoyed strong support.

During World War I, Zákynthos was – like much of Greece – divided into republican and royalist factions. The balance was tipped towards the former by the Entente French, who landed a naval squadron in 1915, followed by a detachment of Senegalese colonial soldiers in early 1917.

The Great Depression hit Zákynthos hard, as it did all over Greece. However, with emigration to the USA restricted by American law after 1924, the islanders mostly had to stay put, or choose Canada instead. In 1935, prior arrivals to California formed the Zakynthian Brotherhood as a mutual aid society; this still exists, though they are now more engaged in organising events than providing aid.

WORLD WAR II AND THE 1953 EARTHQUAKE

As in most of Europe, World War II proved a catastrophe for the Ionians. Although the Greeks initially held off Mussolini's army in 1940–41, driving them deep back into Albania, a more powerful joint German-Bulgarian forces overran Greece during April 1941. Zákynthos, along with all the other Ionian islands, were initially allocated to the Italians but when Italy capitulated to the Allies in September 1943, the Germans replaced them, imposing a far more brutal regime which included the extermination of the Corfiot Jewish community. When they tried to repeat this on Zákynthos, there ensued one of the more heartening episodes of resistance in Nazi-occupied Europe.

THE JEWS OF ZÁKYNTHOS

A Jewish community had been established in Zákynthos Town at least since Venetian times. They were mostly humble craftsmen such as tinsmiths and glaziers, and numbered just 275 persons when the Germans arrived. In October 1943, the Nazis demanded that the local archbishop, Chrysostomos, and the mayor, Loukas Karrer, provide a list of all local Jews within 24 hours. Instead, the pair ordered the islanders to hide the persecuted Jews – mostly out in the countryside. The following day, when the Germans came to retrieve the list from the archbishop and the mayor, they found just two names on it: Karrer and Chrysostomos.

It was a brazenly nervy thing to do, but the Nazis spared their lives, and every one of the island's Jews survived the Nazi occupation in hiding. In 1978, both mayor and bishop had the title of Righteous Among the Gentiles conferred upon them by the Yad Vashem foundation in Israel. The Jewish community was ultimately decimated not by the Nazis but by the 1953 earthquake (see page 23) which caused significant damage and levelled the town's Jewish quarter, including its ornate synagogue.

After this disaster, the first ships to bring aid to the islanders were two Israeli freighters sailing nearby, and subsequently an Israeli naval flotilla. The local Jews expressed their gratitude to their fellow islanders by donating replacement stained glass for the damaged cathedral of Ágios Dhionýsios. But having lost their homes, workshops and place of worship, they then left en masse for either Athens or Israel, where they still maintain a separate synagogue in Tel Aviv. Yet they, or their descendants, still return to their homeland of Zákynthos for holidays.

THE 1953 EARTHQUAKE

Zákynthos had just begun to recover from the joint effects of World War II and the ensuing Greek Civil War

Dhionysios Solomos

when, on 12 August 1953, it was struck by a 6.8 Richter earthquake. The epicentre was on the seabed between Zákynthos and Kefaloniá, so the impact was felt most in the southern, inhabited parts of Kefaloniá, and the relatively unpopulated northern part of Zákynthos. The devastation on Kefaloniá was almost total, with many casualties, while Zákynthos Town – with its Venetian architecture completely unscathed by the war – was also completely destroyed, not just by the quake itself but also by conflagration and explosions, due mostly to escaped cooking fires and the practice of keeping a box of dynamite under the bed to use for illegal fishing. There were relatively few fatalities, although a few looters trapped post-tremor in collapsing houses were unfortunately killed.

Now began new waves of emigration, both internal and overseas (especially to Israel, Australia, Canada, Sudan, the Belgian Congo and South Africa).

THE ARRIVAL OF TOURISM

A period of great post-quake poverty only began to abate when, in 1982, the first package tourists tentatively arrived on the island. Not too much time passed before sparking a wave of indiscriminate tourist development, spreading along the sandy beaches of the south and east coasts. The infamous excesses of Laganás in particular are barely comprehensible to locals; after a murder in a bar brought on by an excess of alcohol, an official was heard to say, "When Greeks get drunk, they get loud and merry – they don't fight or wreck the joint!"

The environmental consequences of tourism have become increasingly evident, and, ironically, it may be the 2016–20 downturn in tourism of almost two-thirds in terms of arrivals that saves the day rather than any proposed green measures by the government.

IMPORTANT DATES

c.50,000 BC Evidence of Palaeolithic settlement.

191BC Acquisition of Zákynthos by the Romans.

AD 337 The islands come under Byzantine rule.

1185–1479 Unopposed Frankish occupation of Ionian islands.

1479 Ottomans overrun Zákynthos, taking many locals prisoner.

1484/1500 Ottomans are expelled from Zákynthos and Kefaloniá by the Venetians, never to return.

1500–1797 Era of Venetian rule leads to the appearance of distinctive churches, sumptuous townhouses and vast olive plantations.

1797 Ionian islands are occupied by the revolutionary French.

1798 Russians and Ottomans, unhappy with Napoleon's agenda, mount a joint expedition and take the islands from the French.

1800 Treaty of Constantinople. The Eptánisos Politía becomes the first autonomous modern Greek state, albeit under Russo-Ottoman control.

1807 Treaty of Tilsit; Ionian islands revert to the Napoleonic French.

1815–64 British occupation of the islands.

1864 Ionian Islands are ceded to Greece upon the enthronement of Greek King George I.

1941–44 World War II. Ionian islands, including Zákynthos, are occupied initially by Italians, then Germans.

1953 Huge 12 August earthquake hits Kefaloniá and Zákynthos, razing most buildings and killing over 400 people.

1982 First package tours arrive on Zákynthos.

2015 Alexis Tsipras becomes Greece's prime minister but is forced to cave in to demands of the country's creditors to avoid bankruptcy.

2016 Greece agrees a rescue deal with creditors, at the price of continued harsh austerity.

2019 Kyriakos Mitsotakis' centre-right New Democracy party wins July elections with outright majority.

2020–21 Covid-19 pandemic shreds two consecutive tourist seasons.

2022 Having demonstrated sustained financial probity, Greece exits its creditors' 'supervision' regime. Record year for tourist arrival numbers.

Cameo Island in Agios Sostis

OUT AND ABOUT

Zákynthos, also known by its Italian name Zante, is the southern-most of the Ionian islands that lie off the western coast of main-land Greece. The island divides into three geographical areas: the Vasilikós Peninsula in the southeast, a central plain extend-ing inland from the east coast, and the wild and mountainous north and west. One of the greenest of all the Greek islands, it has good, fertile soil and receives a generous amount of rain between October and April – typically just under 100cm/40 inches, though global climate change may well affect this pattern.

Although Zákynthos is now thoroughly Greek, evidence of the island's Venetian heritage is inescapable, from its free-stand-ing Italianate church towers to the descendants of aristocratic Venetian families, still major landowners.

ZÁKYNTHOS TOWN

The once-elegant harbour town of **Zákynthos ❶** had its public buildings and squares rebuilt approximately as they were before the devastating 1953 earthquake which decimated much of the infrastructure, but this time in reinforced concrete. Ferries from Kyllíni pull in at the long jetty at the southern end of the harbour, where the port authority can also be found.

Running parallel to the waterfront, three blocks inland, is the main shopping street of Alexándhrou Róma where you will find most of the upmarket boutiques and jewellers. At its north end, Róma meets Platía Agíou Márkou, which adjoins Platía Solomoú, the focus of the northern end of the harbourfront (Lomvárdou, aka Stráta Marína), around which the town's museums and municipal buildings are clustered.

Zákynthos Town

PLATÍA SOLOMOÚ

Platía Solomoú is named after the island's most famous son, the poet Dhionysios Solomos, the father of modernism in Greek literature, who was responsible for establishing demotic Greek (as opposed to the elitist katharévousa form) as a literary idiom. He is also the author of the lyrics to the national anthem, an excerpt from which adorns the statue of Liberty in the square.

Platía Solomoú is home to the massive Museum of Zákynthos and the town **library**, which has a small collection of pre- and post-1953 quake photography. On the seaward corner of the square stands the squat restored church of **Áyios Nikólaos tou Mólou**, where the vestments of St Dhionysios are kept.

THE ZÁKYNTHOS (POST-BYZANTINE) MUSEUM

The **Zakynthos Museum** Ⓐ, Wed–Mon 8.30am–3.30pm), also known as the Post-Byzantine Museum contains many pieces from the old Pandokrátora Museum, as well as frescoes, icons and carvings rescued from churches devastated in the 1953 earthquake. There are also 17th- to 19th-century religious paintings of the Ionian School, founded by Cretan artists fleeing the Ottoman conquest there who met local artists strongly influenced by the Italian

Two-faced island

While Zákynthos's beautiful sandy beaches, concentrated on its southern and eastern coasts, are popular with package holidaymakers, the rest of the island – especially the west coast – remains rugged and, for the most part, undeveloped.

Renaissance. The most prominent island painter was Panagiotis Doxaras (1662–1729).

Start in the room on your right as you go in. Here you will find a wonderful carved ikonostási (altar screen) by Angelos Mosketis (1683). This was rescued from the church of Pandokrátoras (1517), and alongside are photos of the damage to the church caused by the earthquake, and of its reconstruction. The other impressive ikonostási at the end of the room dates from 1690 and is from Ágios Dimítrios tou Kóla (both churches are in Zákynthos Town). There is also a splendid icon of the Panagía from the same church.

As you climb the stairs to the first floor there is a room off to the left that is full of icons. A number of these, on the right, came from the old museum. There are some very fine Venetian-inspired paintings from Agía Ekateríni tou Grypári in Zákynthos Town, and 16th-century icons from Ágio Pnévma in Gaïtáni. Perhaps the most interesting work here is the 17th-century representation of Jerusalem from Agía Ekateríni ton Kípon, Zákynthos Town. Look closely and you will see that this is a very Christian representation of the holy city, with absolutely no evidence of its Muslim heritage to be seen.

Mary Magdalene

Although Greek Orthodoxy concedes that Mary was a virgin, the epithet 'Virgin Mary' is exceedingly rare – heard only in a very few hymns praising the Parthéna María – and Her proper designation in Greek is either Panagía (The All-Holy Female) or Theotókou (God-Bearer, Mother of God).

On the first floor you begin in a small room which contains carved stonework (10th–11th-century), one piece showing the Byzantine double-headed eagle. Then you enter what is possibly the museum's star exhibit: the fabulous, fully frescoed interior of the monastery church of Agíou Andréa in Mesovoúni Volimón. The church itself is 16th century, while the paintings date from the 17th century. The frescoed interior is set out as it was in situ and a number of precious sacred vessels are laid out in front of the apse to indicate the altar.

There follows a long corridor with a display of silver censers. The first bay contains rescued frescoes from the remote monastery of Agíou Georgíou ton Kalogríon (1669); there are also two panels, one of Ágios Nikólaos (St Nicholas) and one of two angels with a scroll, from Agía Ánna (1715). The second bay has a superb series of icons rescued from across the island. Particularly notable are the Panagía i Amólyndos from Ágios Nikólaos tou Mólou, the 17th-century Ágios Ioánnis o Hrysóstomos from Ágios Ioánnis tou Tráfou, and the 17th-century Ascension of the Panagía from the old museum.

The next bay holds late 17th- to 18th-century icons, including a splendid 18th-century specimen of Jonah and the Whale from Ágios Spyrídhonas tou Flambouriári. The final bay is given over to twelve Baroque paintings from the *ikonostasi* of Agíon Anargýron by Nikolaos Koutouzis (1741–1813) and Nikolaos Kantounis

(1767–1834). On the way down the stairs, on the left, are the Kantounis' paintings from the remote monastery of Agíou Georgíou ton Kalogrión.

The final room, on the ground floor, houses a notable model of Zákynthos Town before the 1953 earthquake, giving a good idea of its attractive Italianate character before it was destroyed. On the walls are paintings by Koutouzis from the church of Ágios Spyrídhonas tou Flambouriári.

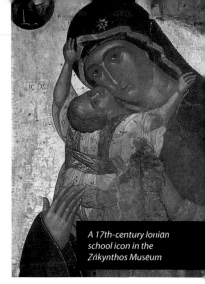

A 17th-century Ionian school icon in the Zákynthos Museum

THE LIBRARY

Next to the town's theatre, also on Platía Solomoú, is the **Library** (winter Mon–Wed noon–7pm, Thu–Sat 8.30am–1pm, summer Mon–Sat 8.30am–2.30pm, also Wed 5–8pm), where there is a small display of photographs showing the pre-1953 island. As well as views of the town and the lavish interiors of some of the island's churches, there are photos of the elegant interiors of the mansions of the Zakynthian Venetian aristocracy, in particular those of the now unfortunately destroyed town palace of the locally prominent Komoutou family.

At the top of the stairs is a small room with a rather bizarre collection of dolls clothed in what purports to be a from of traditional Zakynthian clothing (though strictly speaking there is no such thing).

Home to rest

In 1960 the bodies of Andreas Kalvos and his English wife were brought to Zákynthos from Keddington in Lincolnshire, where the poet had spent much of his life.

Close to the Library, on the corner of the square by the sea, is the reconstructed church of **Ágios Nikólaos tou Mólou**. The attractive stone building is worth a quick visit. However, many of its original icons are now housed in the nearby (Post-Byzantine) Museum of Zákynthos.

THE SOLOMOS/KALVOS MUSEUM

Set back from Platía Solomoú is Platía Agíou Márkou, with a number of cafés, on the far side of which is the **Museum of**

The Solomos/Kalvos Museum

Dionysios Solomos and Eminent Zakynthians B (daily 9am–2pm; https://gozakynthos.gr/museums/museum-of-d-solomos-and-other-eminent-people-of-zakynthos/). Named after Greece's first national poet, the museum is dedicated to famous Zakynthians – these are noticeably male, and in most cases, famous in local terms only. Inside, on the lefthand side, are the rather grand tombs of Solomos and Andreas Kalvos, a fellow poet.

The main body of the museum lies upstairs. The room in front of you is dedicated to a fine icon collection donated by Nikolaos and Thaleia Kolyvos. On the right, a room contains set and costume designs for productions of works by local playwright Dhionysios Romas.

The gallery given over to exhibits on Solomos himself (writer of the lyrics of the Greek national anthem and a champion of Demotic Greek) has a number of portraits, samples of his handwriting and, more bizarrely, a glass urn containing earth from his first grave in Corfu. Visitors might be surprised to notice that many of the manuscripts are in Italian, his first language, rather than Greek. It was only his rising nationalist consciousness which prompted him to begin writing in Greek.

Solomos' Stanzas

Here is a rhyming English translation for the first stanzas of Solomos' 1823 poem "Hymn to Liberty", which in the original runs to 158 verses. The initial stanzas were soon set to music by the Corfiot composer Nikolaos Mantzaros.

I do know thee by the direful cutting edge of thy keen sword
I do know thine eye stare ireful counting fast the lands restored
Thou camest forth off the departed
Greeks who died and lived for thee
and like erstwhile stouthearted
Hail oh hail thee Liberty

Further on, there is an interesting case containing memorabilia of the opera composer and musician Pavlos Karrer (1829–96), otherwise known as Paul or Paulos Carrer. Close by, there is an imposing lithograph of *'The Great Battle of 'Garibaldin' at Siatista under the Leadership of Alexandros Romas'*, next to which is a portrait of Romas himself, bearing a disturbing, and rather uncanny, resemblance to Joseph Stalin.

ÁGIOS DHIONÝSIOS

On the seafront, at the southern end of the harbour, is the most important church – indeed, cathedral – of Zákynthos town, **Ágios Dhionýsios** Ⓒ (daily May–Sept 8.30am–11pm; Oct–Apr 10.30am–2.30pm, 5.30–8.30pm). It was founded by monks previously living in seclusion on one of the Strofádes islands (27 nautical miles

Zákynthos Town at night

south of Zákynthos), where they had been guarding the body of the Zakynthian Ágios Dhionýsios. In 1717, to escape the attacks of pirates, they brought the revered body to Zákynthos and re-established their monastery.

In 1764 the church was remodelled, and a free-standing bell tower was built beside it in 1854. However, the church was completely destroyed in an earthquake in 1893. The present church that stands today – a much sturdier earthquake-proof building, designed by Byzantine scholar Anastasios Orlandos (1887–1979) – was completed in 1948 and was one of the very few buildings to survive the 1953 earthquake on the entire island, only suffering minor superficial damage. An earthquake which wreaked devastating damage on the island.

The church's interior, although modern, is well worth a look. Every inch is covered with paintings and gilding. Around the church, over the tops of the pillars, are a series of panels describing the exploits of the saint, as well as of the relic of his body. One of the more bizarre episodes shows the monks using the desiccated body of the saint to expel a plague of locusts. On the right-hand

Boat trips

At least ten pleasure craft offer day-trips around the island from the quay in Zákynthos Town. All take in sights such as the Blue Caves at Cape Skinári, and moor in Tó Naváyio (Shipwreck Bay) and at the Marathiá caves at Cape Kerí in the southwest. Choose the trip with the most stops, as eight hours bobbing round the coast can become a bore, and check that your operator will actually take you into the caves. Additionally, there are shorter trips to Kerí and turtle-spotting in Laganás Bay, including on one vessel with underwater seating. Cavo Grosso at Lombárdhou 22 (http://cavogrosso.gr) offers a range of excursions.

Zákynthos Town from Bóhali Castle

side of the nave is a small chapel containing the saint's grave. The impressive silver coffin was made in 1829 by Dhiamandis Bafas. He also made the silver surrounds for the icons on the church's intricately carved wooden ikonosási. The saint has two festival periods, celebrated between 23–26 August and 16–17 December.

BÓHALI KÁSTRO

Above the town in the Bóhali district, is the huge Venetian **Kástro D**, or fort (June–Sep daily 8am–8pm; Oct–May, daily 8.30am–3pm; charge). Thought to stand on the site of ancient Psophis (Psophida), the fortress has Byzantine antecedents, but any traces of these earlier settlements – with the exception of the 12th-century Pandokrátor church – have been unfortunately destroyed by earthquakes.

The present fortifications were built under the Venetian *Proveditor General da Mar* Giovanni Battista Grimani and finished in 1646. As a prime defensive site, the fort served as a pirate-proof place of refuge for local people and, particularly during the 17th century, became a flourishing settlement. The fort fell into disuse after 1864, when Zákynthos became part of the Greek Republic.

The Kástro lies at the end of a winding road that leads up from the town through Bóhali hamlet. Just before the top of the hill is the *platía* in front of the church, with a few cafés and tavernas that have a lovely view over Zákynthos Town and harbour. The inside

SONNET – TO ZANTE

Fair isle, that from the fairest of all flowers,
Thy gentlest of all gentle names dost take!
How many memories of what radiant hours
At sight of thee and thine at once awake!
How many scenes of what departed bliss!
How many thoughts of what entombéd hopes!
How many visions of a maiden that is
No more – no more upon thy verdant slopes!
No more! Alas, that magical sad sound
Transforming all! Thy charms shall please no more –
Thy memory no more! Accurséd ground
Henceforth I hold thy flower-enamelled shore,
O hyacinthine isle! O purple Zante!
'Isola d'oro! Fior di Levante!'
Edgar Allan Poe, 1837

of the fort is now a beautiful pine wood, and you have to search around for the remains of the buildings (there is a useful site plan at the entrance). However, perhaps the main reason for coming up to the Kástro is the spectacular panoramic view. The site's slow renovation by the EU and Greek Ministry of Culture has ground to a halt and short off-season opening hours mean sunsets during that period must be enjoyed from one of the many accommodating cafés below.

CENTRAL PLAIN

Zákynthos' central plain is the most fertile in the Ionian Islands. It is mostly given over to intensive cultivation of vines and, away from the coastal resorts and airport, is sprinkled with attractive little villages. Separating the plain from the eastern coast is a line of steep but low hills, while on the western side the mountains rise sharply and dramatically. Along the foot of these mountains lie a string of villages, many located at points where springs emerge from the ridge above.

The central villages include sleepy little Gaïtáni with an attractive Italianate church, and a characteristic separate bell tower, which dates from 1906. Similar architecture can be seen in the neighbouring tiny settlements of Vanáto and Hourhoulídi. The detached bell towers seen across the island are built away from their church to prevent the bells falling through its roof in the event of an earthquake.

On the road between Zákynthos Town and Maherádho is the **Oenolpi Winery** (www.oenolpi.gr). There has been a vineyard

Vines are intensively cultivated in these parts

belonging to the Christoforos family on this spot since 1965 but when they established the Oenolpi Company in 2000, a new modern factory was built that produces some of the best wines on the island. Visitors are invited to tour the estate and the factory, and, of course, to taste/buy the wines (currently four labels of red – including one made from sun-dried Avgoustiátis grapes – rosé and white).

MAHERÁDO, AGÍA MARÍNA AND PIGADHÁKIA

At the foot of the steep climb up to Kiliómeno is the large village of **Maherádho** ❷, home to a couple of interesting churches and some surviving, albeit decaying, examples of traditional pre-earthquake architecture. The village square by the church of Agía Mávra has two nearby cafés serving Greek classics such as *souvláki*, salad and *tzatzíki*.

The main sight in Maherádho was the pilgrimage church of **Agía Mávra and Ágios Timothéos**. The icon of Agía Mávra was supposedly found on this spot and a church built around it. However, a devastating fire in 2005 destroyed the roof and much of the baroque interior by Nikolaos Latsis. Some of the contents were saved and it is still in the process of being restored. The local festival of Agía Mávra, who is said to help healing, is celebrated 18–19 July yearly, though canonically the two saints (who were spiritual companions in life) are honoured on 3 May.

On the left-hand side, just after turning up the hill towards Kiliómeno, is a modern convent whose church has an attractively painted interior. Wrap-around skirts are provided for visitors whose dress is not modest enough for a church visit.

A little southwest of Maherádho, near the village of Lagópodho, lies the Ktima Grampsa winery (tel: 26950 92286; https://ktimagrampsa.gr), run by the brothers Christos and Tassos, whose impressive all-organic production features nearly a dozen white, red and rosé labels. Tours need to be booked by phone or online in advance.

North-northwest of Maherádho, and higher up the mountainside, is the village of **Agía Marína** ❸. The eponymous church has an impressive interior but is often locked. Also here is the **Hélmi Museum of Natural History** (16 Apr–Oct daily 9am–5pm, Nov–15 Apr by appt only; tel: 26950 65040; www.museumhelmis.gr), with a small but informative display on the plethora of flora and fauna on the island.

Further on is **Pigadhákia** ❹, named after its springs (*pigí* in Greek). The lovely 16th-century church of **Ágios Pandelímonas** has an ayíazma (holy spring) in the saint's shrine under the altar, said to promote healing; this is one of the few places where you can go behind the altar screen into the sanctuary, normally

The central plain

reserved for the clergy. The traditional *papadhosiakós* dance is performed at the saint's festival on 27 July.

The **Vertzagio Museum** (Mar–Oct daily 9am–2pm & Sun–Fri 6–8pm, but confirm opening on tel: 2695084077), between Pigadhákia and Katastari, has a motley display of rural artefacts. But it's interesting and worthwhile nonethless.

YERAKÁRI, KYPSÉLI AND TRAGÁKI

Three pretty hilltop villages sit on low hills in the north of the plain. These are **Yerakári**, **Kypséli** and **Tragáki**, the southernmost, largest and most strung out. They all give splendid views over the plain below.

Just 5km (3 miles) southeast of Tragáki, in Sarakinádho, is the **Zante Water Village** (May–Sept hours vary by month; http://zantewatervillage.gr), which is a great family day out. The park offers a variety of waterslides, swimming pools, hot whirlpools, and even a go-kart circuit.

THE EAST COAST

Leaving Zákynthos Town heading north along the seafront, you pass through **Kryonéri**. The water here is reasonably clean, especially considering its proximity to the harbour, and locals swim off the rocks and narrow pebbly beach here. After the steep climb up to pleasant, straggly Akrotíri, the road runs inland along the ridge before descending back down to the sea at **Tsiliví**. This is the first of a string of resorts and not the most pleasant of them. Situated on a lovely bay with a decent beach, Tsiliví is dominated by loud bars, shops peddling tourist souvenirs and holidaymakers grilling red in the sun.

The only conventional attraction here is the **Milanio Maritime Museum** (www.milaniomaritimemuseum.gr). The brainchild of

Laganás

one man, Andonis Milanos, the museum tells the history of Greek seafaring through a series of paintings and model boats, as well as an eclectic assortment of naval artefacts.

Tsiliví blends seamlessly into Plános before things quieten down a bit at Boúka. After the small promontory of Cape Gáidaros, for the next 4km (2.5 miles) between Amboúla and Amoúdi, the road passes turn-offs to a string of small, quiet beaches. There are rooms to rent at most of them, and there are a few excellent beachside tavernas. About 1km (0.6 miles) beyond Amoúdi is **Alikanás**, perhaps the most pleasant of the resorts along this coast. Towards the sea it is still fairly quiet and the mountain backdrop is lovely.

At the northernmost point of the Central Plain sprawls the large resort of **Alykés** ('salt pans' in Greek). A larger version of Tsiliví, Alykés has all the facilities one expects of a Greek package resort – cheap accommodation, all-day English breakfasts and football on satellite TV. It sits, however, on a sweeping bay with a sandy beach and views of Kefaloniá. The exposed bay attracts windsurfers and can generate some surf. This is also one of the places you can take a boat to the Blue Caves near Skinári (trips are advertised everywhere). Behind the town are the old saltworks, the large pans forming shallow lakes where salt was obtained from seawater through evaporation. Since 1980 these are now no longer harvested, as it is cheaper to import salt from the mainland. Consequently, the stagnant water can be rather smelly, though this is home to a wide variety of wildlife; paths take you safely around the salt pond shores.

LAGANÁS BAY

If you dislike mass tourism and loud nightclubs, the place you will most want to avoid on Zákynthos is **Laganás ❺**. Ironically, this – the island's most notorious resort – is right in the middle of its most environmentally sensitive area. It is estimated that these days Zákynthos receives up to 250,000 visitors every year, half of whom stay in Laganás on the south coast. They come for the wonderful sandy beach that stretches from the Vasilikós Peninsula on the northeast to Límni Kerioú beach in the southwest. This lively resort – or den of iniquity, depending on your point of view – is brash,

NATIONAL PARK RULES

Within the confines of the national park, you must not:
- fish
- light a fire
- camp
- pick any plants
- leave any rubbish

LOGGERHEAD TURTLES

The Ionian islands harbour the Mediterranean's main concentration of loggerhead sea turtles, a sensitive species which is under direct threat from the tourist industry. These creatures lay their eggs at night on sandy coves and, easily frightened by noise and lights, are uneasy cohabitants with rough campers and late-night discos. Each year, many turtles fall prey to motorboat injuries, nests are destroyed by bikes and the newly hatched young die entangled in deckchairs and umbrellas left out at night.

The Greek government has passed laws designed to protect the loggerheads, including restrictions on camping on some beaches, but local economic interests tend to prefer a beach full of bodies to a sea full of turtles. On Laganás, nesting grounds are concentrated around the 14km bay, and Greek marine zoologists are in angry dispute with the tourist industry. The turtles' nesting ground just west of Skála on Kefaloniá is another important location, although numbers have dwindled to half their former strength and now only about eight hundred remain. Ultimately, the turtles' best hope for survival may rest in their potential draw as a unique tourist attraction in their own right. The Sea Turtle Protection Society of Greece has a wealth of information about turtle protection programmes and how to volunteer on its website at http://archelon.gr.

The World Wide Fund for Nature has issued guidelines for visitors:
• Don't use the beaches between sunset and sunrise.
• Don't stick umbrellas in the sand in the marked nesting zones.
• Take your rubbish away with you – it can obstruct the turtles.
• Don't use lights near the beach at night.
• Don't take any vehicle onto the protected beaches.
• Don't dig up turtle nests – it's illegal.
• Don't pick up the hatchlings or carry them to the water.
• Don't use speedboats in Laganás Bay – the speed limit is 9km/h.

Yérakas beach, where turtle nests are protected

noisy and nocturnal. Apart from its crowded beach, Laganás' main attraction is its nightlife; one of the more popular daytime spots is the beach-islet of Ágios Sóstis, joined to the shore by a walkway. **Kalamáki**, 4km (2.5 miles) east of Laganás, is perhaps the most pleasant of the hectic resorts on this side of the bay. **Límni Kerioú**, at the southwestern end of Laganás Bay, has gradually evolved into a relaxing and picturesque resort, with a pleasant if not spectacular beach and a couple of diving operations. It's reached by a turning that branches off the main road before it climbs up towards the west coast, after the hill village of Lithakiá.

NATIONAL MARINE PARK

In response to these conflicting demands on the bay – and after intense campaigning by local environmentalists – in 1999 the Greek government established the **National Marine Park of Zákynthos ⑥**, the country's first. The protected area takes in:

the marine area and beaches of Laganás Bay, and around capes Marathiá and Yérakas at either end; an area of land stretching back from the beach, and behind that a buffer zone that extends almost as far as Zákynthos Town; plus the Strofádhes Islands 27 nautical miles to the south. The park's effectiveness has periodically been compromised by funding shortages that can leave it unstaffed and unprotected. Thankfully the crusading Zante Sea Turtle Rescue and Information Centre (see page 50) monitors the situation.

However, the entire bay is the most important nesting site for the loggerhead turtle *(Caretta caretta)* in the Mediterranean basin. The turtles are very sensitive to human disturbance and have suffered greatly from the indiscriminate development of this coast.

The turtles roam throughout the Mediterranean – there is evidence to suggest they use the Gulf of Gabès off Tunisia as a

Marathonisi Island

wintering ground – and in the spring/summer return to Laganás Bay to nest. They rest and mate in the bay while waiting to come ashore during the night. After nightfall, the females crawl up the beach to find a suitable nesting site in the soft sand; if they are disturbed by noise or lights they will return to the sea without laying any eggs. If they are not disturbed, they dig a deep hole and lay a clutch of up to 120

National Marine Park of Zákynthos

eggs, about the size of a ping-pong ball, which take about two months to hatch. The gender of the baby turtles is determined by the ambient temperature in the nest, which in turn is determined by nest depth: 29–30°C results in an even sex balance, with males favoured by lower temperatures, females by higher ones. The eggs take about two months to hatch, after which the hatchlings dig their way to surface and – at night – make their way down to the sea.

Perhaps 1 in 1,000 survive to adulthood; until they attain sufficient size at about 10 years of age, young turtles make easy prey for larger fish, seals and sharks. Loggerheads reach sexual maturity at about 15 years old.

Conflicts with humans arise not only due to pressures of space, forcing the turtles on to fewer beaches and increasing the density of nests, but particularly due to disturbance of the nests themselves (by dogs or foxes as well as humans) and, once the turtles have emerged from their shells, from light pollution. The hatchlings find their way to the sea, only at night, using reflected star- or moonlight on the water. Any shoreside lighting confuses the tiny turtles, causing them to make their way inland, where they will die. By mechanisms not completely understood, these turtles must return to the beach of their birth to reproduce.

The park is home not only to the famous turtles but also, conceivably, the critically endangered Mediterranean monk seal (eleven or twelve of which may still inhabit sea caves just outside of the park), and is important as a rest stop for migrating birds. It also protects certain species of plants, particularly the yellow, fragrant, autumn-blooming sea daffodil *(Pancratium maritimum)* and seabed meadows of Neptune grass *(Posidonia oceania)*, a true vascular plant (not a seaweed) which contributes a large quantity of

The cliffs at Cape Keri

the oxygen in the Mediterranean, and also acts as a critical nursery and shelter for small fish. The habitat of **Lake Kerí** (Límni Kerioú) is the last remaining wetland of Zákynthos, important for migrating bird species. There used to be a huge lake behind Laganás that stretched almost as far as Zákynthos Town, but this was drained to make way for the airport.

THE VASILIKÓS PENINSULA

On the eastern side of Laganás Bay lies one of the most beautiful parts of the island, the **Vasilikós Peninsula**. Heading south from Zákynthos Town the first place you come to is the unappealing resort of **Argási**, sprawling for over a kilometre behind a beach which at certain points narrows to barely 2m/6.5ft in width. As the landscape starts to rise, things begin to improve. Set against the backdrop of Mount Skopós, there are a string of beautiful small beaches along the northern edge of the peninsula. The longest of these, Paralía Iónio, is just seaward from the straggly village of Vasilikós. Iónio verges onto nudist Banana Beach, and around the cape from there is the popular and well established water sports centre at **Ágios Nikoláos**: a free bus service runs here in season from Argási,

Kalamáki and Laganás. The first two coves south of Argási are Kamínia and the more scenic Pórto Zóro. The main road dips and dives along the east coast of the peninsula, with short access roads descending to these and longer beaches further south, such as Iónio and Banana – a free summer bus service runs to both beaches from Zákynthos Town and Laganás. Above these contiguous strands, the only facilities away from the coast are to be found at the rather formless village of Áno Vassilkós. On the opposite side of the bay is some unsympathetic development at Pórto Róma, its name honouring the prominent island family of politicians, diplomats and military men.

The best beach, however, is on the southwestern side at **Yérakas** ❼, a superb sweep of sand fringed by cliffs. There is only one problem – this corner of paradise is an important turtle nesting site. Access en route to Yérakas is controlled by a park ranger, and visitor numbers are strictly limited to protect the nests. For those who want to get even closer to nature, the far end of the beach is nudist.

The exemplary **Zakynthos Sea Turtle Rescue and Information Centre**, operating since 2012 (https://zanteturtlecenter.com/en/), provides information on the turtles and other flora and fauna of the peninsula. They can also advise on joining volunteer environmental protection programmes.

Further back up the peninsula's southwest-facing coast is the isolated beach of Dháfni, with a pleasant *psarotavérna*, reached by a very rough road starting from near Vasilikós village. Between Dáfni and Kalamaki lies the totally protected beach of Sekánia (access only given to scientists with prior permission).

STROFÁHDES ISLETS

The two **Strofádhes (Strofádhia) islets** ❽, Stamfani (Σταμφάνι) and Árpyia (Άρπυια), part of the National Marine Park, form some of the remotest territory in Greece, and make a spectacular,

VENETIAN RUINS

Notable features of the landscape here are ruined stone towers on many hilltops. These are the remains of Venetian windmills, previously used for pumping water up from wells. They are found elsewhere on the island, for example near Cape Skinári, but are especially concentrated near Agalás substantial excursion from Zákynthos. They are located 27 nautical miles south of Cape Yérakas. Currently, Sea Zante on Board (https://seazanteonboard.com/destinations) is the main operator offering such an itinerary from Zákynthos Town; enquire at the small ports of the Vasilikós Peninsula (the closest points to the islets), or in Laganás or Límni Kerioú, for possible alternatives.

On the larger islet, **Stamfáni**, stands a venerable **fortified monastery**, dedicated to the Saviour (Sotíros), established early in the 13th century but taking its present form after a 1440 renovation. A single monk (Grigoris Kladhis, 1937–2017) lived alone out here from 1976 until 2014, but since then there has only been a caretaker for admitting the occasional visitor. Such a visitor may glimpse the original tomb of Ágios Dionýsios, whose remains rested here until being taken to Zákynthos Town in 1717 by monks

The Strofádhes

who were abandoning the monastery in the face of repeated pirate raids; Stamfáni stands only 20m above sea level at its highest point, thus offering little natural protection. In its heyday, Sotíros sheltered more than a hundred monks, who lived from farming the surprisingly fertile islet, even tending citrus orchards. In 2018 a strong earthquake seriously damaged the monastery, which is still awaiting repair.

The only other distinguished structure here is the stone-built **lighthouse** at Stamfáni's eastern tip, dating in its present form from 1887, apart from repaired World War II damage.

Despite their isolation, the Strofádhes were for decades a popular hunting destination, including for a colonel of the 1967–74 military junta who was flown in by helicopter. Since inclusion within the marine park, this activity has obviously ceased, and

Kerí

the islets remain an important nesting and resting stop for more than a thousand species of migratory birds, who delight in the shelter provided by the low juniper groves here. Aside from the monastery, the natural beauty of the place is the main attraction for visitors.

THE HILL VILLAGES AND WEST COAST

The wild and mountainous west coast is the least-spoilt part of the island, with hillsides covered in bright green garigue and maquis (vegetation up to 2.5m high) and small, dry-stone-walled fields. The land falls to the sea in precipitous cliffs, with no easily accessible beaches – one reason why it has resisted tourist development. The sea caves at the foot of the cliffs may still be used for breeding by the very few remaining pairs of Mediterranean monk seals (*Monachus monachus*). This, and the so-far near-pristine environment, are why environmentalists are lobbying for protected status (like that for Laganás Bay) for this region – so far without success. One could argue that it is a fairly pointless endeavour in any case, considering that Greece intends to drill for offshore oil and gas in the sea just west of here as soon as possible.

The hill villages retain much of their traditional architecture and character. Many pre-earthquake buildings survive, though most are too dangerous to live in. One factor that has contributed to their preservation is that no-one can use the damaged buildings unless they have the permission of the owners.

KERÍ, LÍMNI KERIOÚ AND AGALÁS

On the western side of the southern cape – best crossed by the spectacular but rough road from Marathiá hamlet – is the pretty village of **Kerí** **9**, distinguished by its 17th-century church of Panagía Keriótissa. Many of the traditional houses here have been

Odorous beach

The sulphurous smell that wafts around the coast at the tiny bay of Xyngiá – surrounded by steep rock walls – emanates from a hot spring in one of the nearby sea caves.

bought up by German and British visitors, giving the village quite a different, and more reserved, character compared to other places on the island.

Límni Kerioú, was once known for *píssa tou Keríou*, or natural tar pools, mentioned by both Herodotus and Pliny. Now mostly dried up (survivors are walled off and treated as an attraction), they were previously used since antiquity for caulking boats. Just over 1km down the road from upper Kerí is the photogenic lighthouse (built 1925) at Cape Kerí. The two evocatively shaped rock formations in the sea far below to the southeast are called the **Myzíthres**, after an eponymous conical, sweet, soft Greek cheese made from blended sheep and goat cheese.

The minor road north from the village runs through a very attractive wooded valley. It leads to the quiet village of **Agalás**, tucked away in the southwestern part of the island. Next to the church in the centre is a small maritime and natural history museum and art gallery, though, with its erratic opening times, you may have to ask around for the key. Further south into the village, at the point where KTEL buses drop off and pick up, you'll find a café and taverna.

Signposted off from the village are some Venetian wells and the **Damiános cave**, both down towards the sea; the latter can be visited by vehicle and then it's a short walk; there is unrestricted access.

From Agalás head northeast to Lithakiá, where you can get acquainted with the olive oil-making process at the **Aristéon Olive Press and Museum ❿** (www.aristeon.gr). It's a modern working factory where you can learn about the methods of olive oil production and how they have changed over time, see the old machinery and get your questions answered by a very well-informed guide. Of course, you can also taste and buy the olive oil in a range of flavours (the bitter orange is surprisingly good), together with some delicious local bread.

KILIÓMENO AND LOÚHA

At the top of the long, steep climb from Maherádho sits **Kiliómeno** , one of the least earthquake-damaged settlements on Zakynthos. Near the village centre stands the somewhat odd-looking church of Ágios Nikólaos with an unfinished bell tower.

Leaving Kilioméno, the road leads on to the friendly, if slightly lacklustre, village of Áglos Léon. Look out for the Venetian windmill converted into a church tower. A road heading inland from

Agalas Church

here goes up to **Loúha** ⓬, one of the highest, and certainly one of the prettiest, settlements on Zákynthos. The domestic architecture of the hill villages differs from that of the rest of the island; plain exteriors hide attractive courtyards, usually full of flowers, with the living quarters arrayed around them. To get a better look at this arrangement pay a visit to Loúha's tiny village shop and post office (opposite the church of Ágios Ioánnis Theológos). The courtyard behind, with a 400-year-old floor, has an appealing taverna on the first floor. The previously equally attractive village of Gýrio, just beyond Loúha, has been rather spoilt by a breeze-block factory.

The majority of Zákynthos's high mountain villages support the KKE (Greek Communist Party). The Communists have organised collective agricultural cooperatives to help local farmers buy machinery, and then harvest and market their produce. More recently, the party has been involved in local campaigns against the installation of more wind turbines on the island. From Ágios Léon a pretty but winding, and initially very narrow, road leads down to seaside **Limniónas**. There is really nothing here but a taverna that looks out over a beautiful rocky bay. Beside the taverna a steep flight of steps leads down to a small bathing platform.

ÉXO HÓRA TO ANAFONÍTRIA

The main road carries on north to **Éxo Hóra**. At the crossroads at the village centre is a huge olive tree, reputedly the oldest on the island. This crossroads is also the turn-off for **Kambí**, where a large concrete cross glowers down on the sea from a tall headland, atop the cliffs of Skhíza. The cross commemorates the spot from where right-wing soldiers threw a group of local Communists to their death during the civil war, or vice versa, depending whose version of the story you believe. It seems that the second theory is more likely; at some point during the left-wing PASOK governments of the 1980s, an explanatory plaque to that effect was removed.

Anafonitria Monastery

The unspoilt village of **Mariés** lies 5km further north. Local legend claims Mary Magdalene landed here to spread the Gospel. This may account for what seems to be a disproportionate number of churches for the village's rather small size (300 inhabitants) – including one dedicated to Mary Magdalene – but not for the derivation of the name, which is probably a corruption of mouriés or mulberry trees.

Beyond Mariés and Orthoniés villages to the east, towards the coast, the Gkoumas Estate (tel: 26951 00431 or 6944 326679; https://artandwine.gr) hosts both an innovative winery and an icon workshop with some icons painted by Yannis Giatras-Gkoumas for sale. Wine products include four whites, four reds and a rosé, including a few made from sun-dried grapes.

Where the road turns east towards the village of Orthoniés, there is a turn left for **Anafonítria** village and monastery **13**. Ágios Dhionýsios was abbot at the 14th-century monastery from 1578 until his death in 1622. Further on, above the turn for Navágio, lies the 16th-century monastery of **Ágios Geórgios ton Krimnón**, with a striking round lookout tower in its tidy courtyard.

NAVÁGIO (SHIPWRECK) BAY

Just beyond Anafonítria is the headland overlooking **Navágio Bay** (Shipwreck Bay) ⑭ – an extremely sheltered bay where a dilapidated freighter lies half-buried in sand. It is the most photo-graphed beach in Zákynthos, if not the entire Ionians, and appears on numerous posters and postcards. The wreck has been here since 2 October 1980, driven ashore by a combination of engine failure and foul weather; it was allegedly engaged in smuggling contraband cigarettes from Tunisia to Italy or Greece. Until 2022 it was perhaps the most popular sea-going excursion on the entire

Shipwreck Bay

island, but since a landslide that summer caused by a 5.4-magnitude earthquake made the lovely beach unsafe to disembark upon, visitors were forbidden to reach the beach by boat and subsequently blocked access to the beach by road. Since then, tourist numbers to site have fallen but actions are being taken to make it safer to visit.

Additionally, after 40-plus years of exposure to the elements, the wreck is now unsound; well before the landslide, plans were announced to consolidate it against creeping rust.

Looking down the sheer cliffs from the small steel-viewing platform above is quite spectacular and, for anyone with even a mild distrust of heights, quite stomach churning. Landslips permitting, boat trips shuttle sightseers to the beach from **Pórto Vrómi**, below Mariés. The bigger operators are perhaps best avoided for environmental reasons; boats above a certain size are not supposed to land on the beach, but they will often flout the rules and invariably do.

THE NORTH

Beyond **Alykés**, as you approach the island's tip at **Cape Skinári**, the coast becomes more rugged, while the mountains inland hide the weaving centre of **Volímes** ⓯. Divided into three contiguous parts, Volímes is the centre of the island's embroidery industry and numerous shops sell artefacts produced here. With your own transport, you could make it to the Anafonítria monastery, 3km south, thought to have been the cell of the island's patron saint, Dhionysios, whose festivals are celebrated on August 24 and December 17.

Alykés Bay, 12km north of Tsiliví, is a large sandy bay with lively surf and the northeast's two largest resorts. The first, **Alikanás**, is a small but expanding village, and much of its accommodation is foreign-owned villa rentals. The second, **Alykés**, named after the spooky saltpans behind the village, has the best beach north of the capital.

North of Alykés the landscape becomes more desolate, rugged and deserted. It was this part of the island that felt the strongest tremors during the 1953 earthquake; the epicentre was in the channel between northern Zákynthos and Kefaloniá.

The long climb out of **Katastári** (the largest village outside the capital) gives views back to Alykés Bay and over to Kefaloniá. After passing the 16th-century Ioánnou Prodrómou monastery, with an important icon by Cretan master Theodore Poulakis (1622–92), you reach the turn-off for Mariés. The road that continues over to the west coast passes through some stunning scenery.

The road along the east coast then plunges down a very steep (10 percent) hill, passing by **Xyngiá** ⑯ and around a headland indented by numerous sea-caves, to the beach at **Makrýs Yialós**. Here, there are several places to eat and sea-caves you can swim into right by the beach. About 500m (550 yards) further on is the tiny headland of **Mikrónisi,** where you can eat at the single taverna overlooking boats bobbing in the small inlet – some of these can be rented through the local rental franchise (https://mikronisi.com) and used to explore the area from the sea. Beyond here is the turn-off for the three contiguous districts of **Volímes** village, famous for their honey and textiles, as well as their surviving traditional mountain architecture.

The road hugs the coast from here to the small port of **Ágios Nikólaos** ⑰, where there are at least daily May–Sept ferries to Pesáda harbour on Kefaloniá, but it is best to get boats to the **Blue Caves** ⑱ from just below the spectacularly perched, stone-clad, 1897-built lighthouse at Cape Skinári, the extreme northern tip of the island. The water in the caves appears bright blue, and seems to colour your skin as you swim.

The Blue Caves

Crystal clear water perfect for swimming

THINGS TO DO

SPORTS

The wonderfully clear sea of Zákynthos invites visitors to do more than just sit in a deck chair or sunbed looking out at the view. Options for active holidays are numerous, ranging from swimming, diving and sailing to walking, cycling and horse riding.

WATER SPORTS

Swimming. The water quality around Zakynthos is excellent. The water is extremely clear and clean, with swimming season notionally from late April to late October, though the less hardy may prefer late May through early October. For small children, the southern and eastern beaches (for example Kalamáki, Pórto Koúkla near Límni Kerioú and Tsiliví) are best, as they have gently sloping sand bottoms, are generally more shallow and have calm waters. Otherwise, most hotels and many apartments have swimming pools, though in mid-summer it would be a shame not to take advantage of the warm sea (up to 27°C) surrounding the island.

Boat hire

Hiring a small (25 horse-power) motorboat is the best way to explore secluded, otherwise inaccessible bays. They are available from travel agents in many places and cost about €150 per day plus petrol; Zakynthos Boat Rentals (tel: 6971 621408, https://zanteboats.com/prices-reservation/) is one such company. The boats offer great opportunities for swimming – simply anchor, then dive or jump off the side; all boats have a fold-down ladder to help you get back on board.

Snorkelling and scuba-diving. The coasts around Zákynthos are a divers' paradise – the rocky shoreline is home to wide variety of creatures, and the calm, clear water permits visibility of up to 50m (164ft). All scuba-diving schools have qualified instructors who will choose dive locations according to your experience. Extended boat trips are available for advanced divers. For the more advanced trips, or to hire equipment and go by yourself, you will need to show an appropriate diving certification card. Several major resorts have reputable diving schools.

Well-regarded dive centres on Zákynthos, listed below, are approved by the Professional Association of Diving Instructors (PADI; www.padi.com). At Diving Center Turtle Beach in Límni Kerioú (tel: 29650 49424 or 6944 375597; https://diving-center-turtle-beach.com), prices for qualified divers start from €45 per dive with equipment supplied; per-dive prices drop for multiple dive packages. Courses are also offered, starting at €295 for an Advanced Open Water certification for those who already have the basic Open Water Diver qualification. Also recommended at Límni Kerioú is 1986-established Nero Sport Dive Centre (tel: 26950 28481, www.nero-sport.de), offering multi-dive packages and

YACHTING

The relatively calm and safe waters around Zákynthos, coupled with the wonderful marine environment, have made this area very popular with yacht owners and companies running bareboat charter and flotilla holidays. Companies that charter boats out of Zákynthos or run flotillas calling there include: Sunsail (www.sunsail.com), Zakynthos Private Yachting (https://zakynthosprivateyachting.com), based in Zákynthos Town Marina, and Patras Yachts (www.patrasyachts.gr/zakynthos).

Cave diving

certification courses. Coastal Diving Centre is a good east-coast choice in Tsiliví (https://www.coastaldc.gr/index.php/en).

For advanced divers, the single most exciting destination is the wreck of the Perseus, a British submarine which sank on 6 December 1941 after hitting an Italian mine in the channel between Zákythos and Kefaloniá; it now rests at a depth of 52m. Similarly challenging and attractive is diving the wreck of the passenger-and-freight ferry Zakythnos, which sunk in a violent September 2017 storm between the island and Kyllíni port on the Peloponnesian mainland when its cargo shifted abruptly, and now lies 42m down. If you don't want to engage in full-scale scuba diving, snorkelling with simply a mask, snorkel and flippers can be nearly as rewarding.

Water sports. Zákynthos is an excellent island to visit for organised water sports, with major centres located at Tsiliví, Alykés and Ágios Nikólaos on the Vasilikós Peninsula, where St Nicholas Beach

Watersports (https://zakynthoswatersports.gr/watersports) at Ágios Nikólaos beach on the Vasilikós Peninsula focuses on passive motorised activities such as parasailing, banana boating and ringo rides (they also offer scuba diving). Equipment for windsurfing is available for hire at certain beaches and instruction is offered at many places. Parasailing, which is now very popular, is available at a number of Zakynthian beaches, as is jet-skiing.

WALKING

Zákynthos not only has a wonderful shoreline but also a beautiful interior with some walking opportunities, not all of them strenuous. One locally based (Alykés) specialist organising tours is Zakynthos Experience (tel: 26950 83344, https://zakynthosactivities.com/experiences/hiking-tours-zante).

HORSE RIDING AND CYCLING

These are both excellent ways of seeing Zákynthos. Laganás Horse Riding, on the road between Laganás and Kalamáki resort, arranges riding excursions both inland and along turtle-free beaches. Other centres recommended for their customer service and attention to animal welfare are Paraskhis Zakynthian Horse Stud, aka Yannis Horses (Alikanás, tel: 6937 061259 or 6975769091, www.facebook.com/Parashis-Zakynthian-Horse-StudYannis-horses-347446518669800) and Rodeo Alykés Horse Riding (Alykés, tel: 6979 013287, https://web.facebook.com/rodeoalykeshorseriding). All of these stables offer as an option the chance to ride in shallow sea on your mount.

Podilatadiko Cycling Center Zakynthos (tel: 6942 407167, https://podilatadiko.com/en-bike-rentals/), based at Koutoúzi 88 in Zákynthos Town, is the place for either independent rentals of mountain or road/racing bicycles, or to join four escorted touring routes. Many of the minor roads are relatively quiet, but take great care on the main coastal roads. Except for the westerly mountainous ridge, grades are usually gentle.

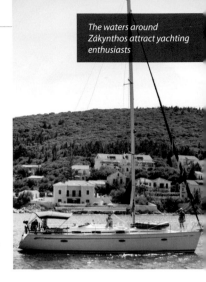

EXCURSIONS BY KAÏKI (CAIQUE)

Popular boat trips on Zákynthos are to the Blue Caves at Cape Skinári to Navágio Beach - take the kaïki from the lighthouse at the cape, ignoring the touts at Ágios Nikólaos port itself – or, most adventurously, to the Strofádhes islets. There is also a plethora of all-day round-the-island trips. Take your pick from the harbour of Zákynthos Town.

ENVIRONMENTAL VOLUNTEERS

One of the best, and most rewarding, ways of seeing Zákynthos is to volunteer on an environmental protection programme run by one of the local eco-groups. On Zákynthos much of the work is dedicated to safeguarding the nesting loggerhead turtles on Laganás Bay and to protecting the environment of the National Marine Park.

Several organisations are involved in this work; the park authority itself is supposedly setting up a voluntary scheme, but the longest-established organisation on Zákynthos is the Sea Turtle Protection Society of Greece (https://archelon.gr), which runs turtle protection programmes and other ecological activities for guests, upon payment of a participation fee.

SHOPPING

Prices are rising in Greece in line with considerable inflation and, as a result, you shouldn't expect to find any great bargains on Zákynthos. In souvenir and gift shops you might find that some good-natured bargaining is tolerated if you are buying more than one item or spending a substantial amount, but don't push your luck. Local profit margins have to cover not only operations during the tourist months but also the off-season, when most of the shops are closed.

If you are not a resident of the EU, you might be able to claim back the 24 percent VAT (sales tax) included in the price of most goods if you spend over a certain amount. Ask for details at shops sporting 'Tax-Free for Tourists' stickers.

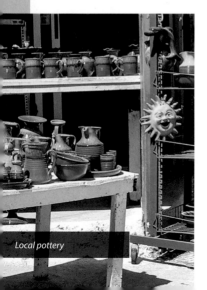

Local pottery

WHAT TO BUY

Truth be told, Zákynthos is not a shoppers' paradise, and the best things to buy as gifts or mementos of your trip are consumables such as olive oil, thyme honey and local sweets (see page *xx*). The island produces a selection of fine wines, such as the white Popolaro, as well as sugarshock-inducing *mandoláto* nougat, Amongst the touristic merchandise peddled in the resorts, from inflatable turtles and novelty key rings to mass-produced figurines of turtle hatchlings, you'll have to look hard to find anything worth bringing home. An exception to this is gold or silver jewellery, which can be of very good quality and made in attractive, unusual designs. Zákynthos Town is a good place to start: try either Savvas (tel: 26950 23688, www.facebook.com/savvasgoldsmiths/) or Platinum (tel: 26950 25044), both of which are on pedestrianised Platía Agíou Márkou.

Another item worth looking out on the island for is a decent, skilfully executed reproduction icons. These are widely available, but the best ones tend to be on sale at museum shops and monasteries – or at the Gkoumas Estate (see page 57).

Leather items, especially handmade bags and sandals, can be good buys but you might want to shop around for the best quality and selection.

Ceramics are among the few artisanal items worth bringing home and Zákynthos has some excellent craft potters, both at the main resorts and in the smaller inland villages. You may also consider buying hand-embroidered textiles; the women's cooperative in Volímes has an excellent reputation.

NIGHTLIFE

There are considerable differences in the nightlife across Zákynthos. For the most part, this is divided into two broad types: that which is more traditionally Greek, in particular the authentic evenings in tavernas listening to Ionian kandádhes, or their local variant arékia, through to the heavily tourist-orientated 'Greek nights' that revolve around clubs in the resorts.

If the latter is your thing, then head for Laganás, which has many nightclubs, including Rescue Club (http://rescueclub. net), supposedly Greece's largest club outside Athens. Other places to check out include Zeros (https://zerosclubzante.com/

contact-zeros-club-zante/) and the Cameo Club, which is on the islet of Ágios Sóstis, accessible across a walkway from the beach, though this has mostly re-invented itself as a daytime family-beach-bar destination. Elsewhere on Zákynthos, the clubs outside Argási are pretty lively, while those in Tsiliví and Alykés are a bit more staid. At Límni Kerioú, Rock Café is a durable favourite for cocktails, ice cream and regular DJ events, with views out to Marathonísi; their snack dishes are fairly forgettable, though breakfasts are pretty good.

GREEK NIGHTS

Whichever resort you are staying in on Zákynthos, you may come across a 'Greek Night', which generally comprises a fairly traditional meal, music (usually live) and dancing. It is, of course, the last of these that everyone comes to see. Traditional Greek dances are taught from an early age, and the dancers – be they specially hired performers, restaurant staff or simply locals who want to strut their stuff – can almost always be relied upon for an energetic performance.

Whereas some Greek island dances are quite low key, Zakynthian men revel in athletic, fast dances with high-kicking, Cossack-like steps and lots of bravado; dancing inside a ring of fire is quite typical. Another dance involves picking up a glass of wine with the mouth (no hands allowed) from a press-up position. Then, the entire glass of wine is swallowed in one gulp with a jerk of the neck. Another crowd pleaser is the solo *zeïbékiko*, traditionally a male preserve, but Greek women have recently begun to execute this style too. The spectators, clapping in time to the music, cheer on the dance. By the end of the night, it is a fair bet that the dancers will have cajoled everyone up on to the floor to join in a version of the *syrtáki*, Greece's best-known line dance; the steps are simplified for visitors.

These dances are usually all accompanied by the bouzoúki, the famous four-double-stringed fretted long-necked lute which for many foreigners has become synonymous with all Greek music. In fact, the instrument (which is of Middle Eastern origin) is a comparatively recent import to the island, though the haunting melodies of Manos Hatzidakis and Mikis Theodorakis have made bouzoúki music an intrinsic part of pan-Hellenic folklore.

CHILDREN

It is easy to travel with a family in Greece, and Zákynthos in particular is a popular destination for those with children. The Greeks are very tolerant – not to say out-and-out indulgent – of children; it is common to see local youngsters late at night in tavernas, learning

There are many waterparks on Zante

early on the circadian rhythms of their elders – eating, playing tag and tormenting the cats under the tables, while visitors' children will be accepted doing the same. In addition, many of the larger and more expensive hotels and resorts have facilities for children, either full-on kids' clubs or just play areas and dedicated, shallow swimming pools. Children will be more than happy to visit the Zante Water Village (at Sarakinádho, 3km southeast of Tragáki; http://zantewatervillage.gr; open May–Sept, hours vary by month), a waterpark with a variety of waterslides, swimming pools, warm whirlpools and even a go-kart circuit.

The active, outdoor life should appeal greatly to those with an adventurous spirit, with the beach being the obvious focus of activities. For older children, the Blue Caves are excellent for snorkelling, and when you dive off the boat into the water, your skin will appear bright blue. Budget-friendly boat trips depart from Cape Skinari. Opt for a combined tour with Shipwreck Bay, where you can see the remains of a cargo ship that was mistaken for a drug-running vessel and run aground by the coastguard in the 1960s. Do remember, however, that the Mediterranean sun is very strong and that children can burn easily and quickly. Make sure they wear a T-shirt and use a high-factor sunscreen.

On Zákynthos, there are two trenákia (road trains) that might appeal to children. One runs frequently between Zákynthos Town and Argási, while another (https://trainaki.com) goes from Alykés in a half-loop inland through the nearby countryside and villages, ending at Alikanás. Trekking on horseback is also a possibility (see page 66 for recommended stables), though this is not one for very young children.

Activities centred around wildlife can also be popular. Boat trips with a chance of glimpsing swimming turtles and visits to the natural history museum are other possible excursions that will go down well with kids.

CALENDAR OF EVENTS

1 January New Year's Day (*Protohroniá*). Feast Day of Ágios Vasilios (St Basil). Before Western ideas of Santa Claus became widespread in Greece, this was the traditional day on which gifts were exchanged.

6 January Epiphany (*Agía Theofánia or Fóta*). In sea-, river- or lakeside parishes the priest or bishop blesses the waters by throwing in a crucifix into the water, then young men dive to retrieve it. Whoever succeeds gets immediate kudos, and good luck for the year ahead.

Easter The great festival of the Greek calendar. A moveable feast comprising several parts: **February/March**, *Apókries*, the period before Lent that is Greece's carnival season; Tsikhnopémpti, 'Grilled Meat Scent Thursday', when all *psistariés* are packed out for a final carnivorous dinner; **Clean Monday**, the first day of Orthodox Lent (*Kathará Deftéra*), when in good weather everyone goes out for a picnic, **Good Friday**, biers (*epitáfii*) of Christ from each parish church are taken on evening procession; **Easter Sunday**, at midnight on the Saturday the priest announces that Christ has risen and passes the flame of eternal life from the *ierón* (sanctuary) to the candles of the congregation. What follows is celebrations with music and dance.

25 March Independence Day.

1 May May Day. Workers' parades and excursions to the countryside to gather flowers and greenery for May wreaths, which are hung on front doors until traditionally burnt on St-John's-Eve (23 June) bonfires.

3 May Feast of Agía Mávra, Maherádho, Zákynthos.

23–26 August Feast day of Ágios Dhionýsios (patron saint of the island), Zákynthos Town (also 16–17 December).

28 October *Óhi* Day. Celebration of the 1940 Greek refusal to accept Mussolini's ultimatum, triggering Greece's resistance to Italy's invasion.

25 December Christmas Day; the 26th is also an official holiday.

31 December *Paramoní tis Protohroniás* (New Year's Eve). Most housewives bake a *vasilópita* (cake in honour of St Basil); a coin is secreted inside, and the one whose slice it turns up in gets good luck for the year. Adults play cards for money.

FOOD AND DRINK

At its best, Greek food is delicious, fresh and well prepared; olive oil, tomatoes, onion, garlic, cheese and lemon are all essentials of a simple cuisine. Take an idyllic waterside setting, add charcoal-grilled fish, meat on a spit and a crisp salad, and you have the staples of a typical Greek meal.

Traditionally, a restaurant *(estiatório)* does not have entertainment; it is a place for straightforward eating. *Estiatória* (plural) typically provide *magireftá*, oven-cooked or stovetop-casserole dishes that you choose by entering the kitchen and indicating what you want. Tavernas are more social establishments where customers may spend an entire evening drinking and eating; *psarotavérnes* specialise in fish and seafood. A *psistariá* has rotisserie and flat grills for cooking meats and poultry.

In beach resorts, the taverna – with mostly outdoor seating, and thus usually shut from late October to early May – reigns supreme. ordering by sight is not the rule, except when choosing scaly fish from a chiller case. But neither should you rely on menus – many of these are wishful thinking, issued free to the establishment by a sponsoring drinks company, listing dishes that are

Lamb moussaka

never offered. The only reliable bill of fare will be recited by your waiter; check the menu only to verify prices. These include service charge, but diners normally leave 5 to 10 percent extra for the waiter unless service has been abysmal. A cover charge includes bread, which varies in quality – darker village bread is excellent. You may decline it if you like as it is no longer obligatory, and many waiters have begun asking foreigners if they actually want bread; look at other diners' tables to see what's being provided.

> ### Some like it hot
>
> *Magireftá* food is served lukewarm and with lots of olive oil, both considered to promote good digestion. For hot food, ask for it *zestó*; food without oil is *horís ládhi*. However, both such requests will be considered eccentric. Casserole dishes such as *moussakás* are cooked for lunchtime and either kept warm all day or just microwave-reheated at night. If you like your food hot or if you are concerned about the hygienic implications of re-heating, order only grilled, fried or marinated dishes in the evening.

Islanders have lunch between 2.30 and 4pm, dinner from 9.30pm onwards, with some establishments taking last orders as late as 11.15pm. Tavernas aimed at foreigners begin dinner service at around 7pm; you will have your choice of table then, but the atmosphere is definitely better later on.

FAST (STREET) FOOD

For snacks or even lunch, pop into a bakery for a *tyrópita* (cheese-filled *filo* pastry pie); the *filo*-less version looking like a turnover, called *kouroú*, is less messy and more cheese-filled; if it's stuffed with spinach, it's a *spanakópita*.

Meats (almost always pork chunks, rarely lamb) grilled on a small skewer are called *souvláki*, while *gýros* are thin slices of pork

Tzatzíki

cut from a vertical rotisserie spit; both are served with garnish, a pinch of chips and *tzatzíki* on pita bread.

MEZÉDHES, OREKTIKÁ AND SALADS

Mezédhes or *orektiká* (appetisers) are small plates of starter food, either cold or hot; carefully selected combinations of *mezédhes* or *orektiká* can constitute a full meal. Shared by the whole table, they are a fun way to eat – you have as little or as much as you want and keep ordering until you have had your fill.

The most common appetisers are *tzatzíki*, a yoghurt dip flavoured with garlic, cucumber and mint; *dolmadhákia*, vine leaves stuffed with rice, onions and herbs, which can be served hot (with egg-lemon sauce) or cold (with dollops of yoghurt). Mince only appears in *lahanodolmádhes* (stuffed cabbage leaves). Fried *kolokythóanthi* (stuffed squash blossoms) appear in summer and early autumn, sadly often coated in heavy batter; the filling is usually herb-flecked rice. Pale (preferably not pink) *taramosaláta*, fishroe paste, is served blended with breadcrumbs, olive oil and lemon juice; *aliáda*, similar to the *skordhaliá* garlic purée found elsewhere in Greece, is found on Zákynthos but made with potatoes rather than breadcrumbs, and served with fried vegetable slices or battered *galéos* (baby dogfish shark); *melitzanosaláta*, a purée of grilled aubergine, onions, olive oil and garlic, much preferably *nistísimo* (without mayonnaise); *tyrokafterí*, a chilli-spicy cheese dip. *Tyropitákia* are small pastry parcels filled with cheese (be wary of defrosted catering-pack ones, as opposed to home-made), while *pastourmadópita* are similarly-sized pastry parcels filled with Armenian-style cured beef. *Keftedhákia* are small, fried meatballs bound with breadcrumbs and perhaps egg, flavoured with coriander and spices, but *kolokythokeftéedhes* are fried croquettes based on courgettes/zucchini. *Saganáki* is a hard cheese slice coated in breadcrumbs and fried, though confusingly the term can also mean a cheese-based red sauce dousing mussels and shrimp.

Greek salad or *horiátiki saláta* (usually translated as 'village salad') consists of tomato, cucumber, onion, green peppers and olives topped with feta cheese. During the cooler spring months, you may be offered a salad of finely shredded lettuce (*maroúli*) with spring onions and dill. *Ambelofásola*, steamed or boiled green/runner beans, available from July into September, are considered a salad in Greece, as are *kolokythákia* (courgettes) boiled whole and served drowned in olive oil, and *hórta*, notionally boiled wild chicory greens but in mid-summer most likely to be cultivated amaranth leaves (*vlíta*), served lukewarm or at room temperature, again with oil and vinegar or lemon. Come autumn, cabbage/carrot salad (*lahanokaróto*) appears, often with too much cabbage

Souvláki

Taverna in Zákynthos town

and not enough grated carrot. All salads should arrive at the table dressed with olive oil and vinegar. If you require more oil, a pre-covid law requires sealed, mini-bottles of oil to be provided (and charged extra for), though enforcement of this rule has become lax. Cruets of bulk olive oil and wine vinegar may still be found with other condiments on the table, attached to the napkin rack, though since the advent of Covid-19, salt and pepper shakers may be replaced with tiny paper packets, and silverware is often provided in a paper sleeve containing precisely one paper napkin (you may ask for more if there isn't a condiments rack on the table).

MAIN COURSES: MEATS AND CASSEROLES

Common oven dishes include *moussakás* (minced meat, aubergine and potato slices with béchamel sauce and a cheese topping), brought to Greece by refugees from Asia Minor, but with ultimate origins in the Arab world; and *pastítsio* (macaroni and mincemeat pie topped with béchamel sauce – an obvious Italian borrowing). *Kléftiko* is Cypriot-style lamb, slowly baked until it is very tender, while *stifádo* is beef or rabbit braised with pearl onions. *Briám* or *tourloú* (a ratatouille of potatoes, tomatoes and courgettes) and *fasolákia laderá* (green beans *yahní*) are two other popular casserole dishes, while *fasoláda* (white bean soup) is a winter favourite. Springtime treats, if you coincide with them, are *angináres* (artichokes) – you may find the spinier but very tasty wild ones on Zákynthos – but usually only available year-round as defrosted hearts in *angináres ala políta* (stewed in a white broth with potatoes and carrots), and *koukiá* (fresh broad beans, May only; otherwise they are rehydrated). *Bámies* (okra) are also particularly good, most commonly served during mid-summer in a red sauce. For a more substantial hot meatless dish, *gemistá* are tomatoes or peppers stuffed with herb-flavoured rice (though meat stock may be used); alternatively, *melitzánes imám* (aubergine/eggplant richly prepared with tomato, onions and oil) is reliably vegetarian, as are *yígandes* (pale haricot beans in tomato sauce).

Sit-down barbecued dishes include whole chickens or *kondosoúvli* (rotisserie-grilled pork), possibly only available at weekends when the local clientele makes it worthwhile for the taverna-keeper to light an enormous bank of coals. If you want a basic pork cutlet, ask for a *brizóla*; a veal chop is a *spalobrizóla*; lamb or goat chops, however, are *païdhákia*. *Souvláki* is also served as a main sit-down course in tavernas and *psistariés*, as are *pantsétes*, not quite Italian belly bacon (*pancetta*) but resembling more American spare ribs. *Biftékia*, grilled or baked 'hamburgers', sometimes stuffed with rich cheese for extra artery-clogging properties, are ubiquitous. *Yiouvétsi* is beef or lamb chunks, *kritharáki* (orzo pasta) and tomato sauce cooked in a covered, often ceramic pot. *Soutzoukákia* are minced-meat rissoles cooked in a red sauce. *Yiouvarlákia* are mincemeat-and-rice balls covered

Grilled sardines

in egg-and-lemon sauce *(avgolémono)* or swimming in a thinner broth. More unusual foods you may encounter include *kokorétsi* (lamb's offal wrapped in intestines and grilled over a spit), or sheep/pork testicles, known as 'unmentionables' *(amelétita)*. If you are on Zákynthos at Easter, you may break the Lenten fast with the islanders just after Saturday midnight with tasty *mayirítsa*, a soup made from finely chopped lamb's offal and dill. Whole spit roasted lamb (or goat) is the main feature of Easter Sunday midday outings.

DESSERTS

Desserts are not usually on the menu except in the most touristy eateries – think panna cotta or tiramisu – but often offered on the house with the bill as a *kérzama* (sweet treat). Those you are most likely to be given, besides the two just cited, include yoghurt with honey, often with walnut pieces; *simigdalísios halvás*, made with semolina; *kormós*, a chunk of chocolate loaf; or *glyká tou koutaliou*, 'spoon' sweets, candied fruit, usually grapes or cherries. Sometimes you will encounter *galaktoboúreko*, filo pastry filled with custard and topped by syrup; *baklavás*, made of crushed nuts in filo pastry, again with syrup; *karydhópita*, walnut cake, or *ravaní*, sponge cake, either of these doused in varying amounts of syrup. During midsummer, the *kérazma* may only be a plate of the most abundant seasonal fruit: grapes, figs, chunks of Persian melon or watermelon. For something more unhealthily sweet, a *zaharoplastío* (sticky-cake shop) offers decadent oriental sweets: *baklavás*, as described above; *kataïfí*, 'shredded wheat' filled with chopped almonds and honey; or *galaktoboúreko* as above. Quality ice-cream, including proper gelato, has arrived in Greece with a vengeance. Anywhere with many Italian tourists (including Zákynthos) should support at least one passably genuine gelateria, possibly even Italian-owned and staffed.

SEAFOOD AND FISH

Fish sizes vary from the tiny picarel *(marídhes)* and summertime sardines (*sardhéles*) or sand smelt *(atherína)*, to the larger dentex *(synagrída)*, swordfish *(xifías)* or dusky grouper *(rofós)*. In between are red mullet *(barboúni)* or the smaller, less expensive, related goatfish *(koutsomoúra)* and several breams (*tsipoúra, fangrí, sargós* and *melanoúri*). Fresh hake *(bakalarákia)* is much esteemed, as is *galéos*, a type of small shark. Fresh scaly fish is sold by weight (before it is cleaned) and you might want to keep an eye on the scales; also look out for fish marked *katapsygméno* (frozen), sometimes just withan asterix, 'kat' or 'k' on menus. Larger fish is usually grilled and smaller fish fried, though sardines are ideally grilled, then served *petáli* (butter-flied) and deboned. Staff can sometimes be reluctant to agree to grilling, claiming that the too-small specimen

Psarotavérnes

These can be very expensive but will have some fresh fish unless winds have kept the boats in harbour, or it's the heart of closed season (June–Sept) when mega-trawlers and other drastic fishing methods cannot be used. A good rule of thumb to guarantee fresh, not defrosted, fare is to only order seasonal fish.

Exotic Cuisine

If you tire of local fare, you can usually find everything from gourmet cuisine to foreign fare, from Chinese stir-fry to crêpes. Don't turn your nose up at Italian food in particular – the Greeks love pizza and pasta, and the numerous Italian visitors demand high standards.

will fall apart; insist. The most common big species, served with fresh lemon and *ladolémono* (a cruet of olive oil with lemon juice), are listed in our menu reader. Lemon wedges are also served with your fish, though rarely enough – you may ask for more, free. Grilled octopus (*htapódi*) and cuttlefish (*soupiá*) are delicious, and deep-fried squid (*kalamarákia*), though usually defrosted from a supermarket pack, are often available. *Gónos* (hatchling) may refer to baby whole squid, or to any small fish. You may also find Aegean lobster (*astakós*), not a true homardian species, soften flaked and cooked with spaghetti (*astakomakaronádha*) but occasionally grilled.

WHAT TO DRINK

In the summer you will need to drink a lot of water, but do try to avoid bottled 'spring' water, as Greece's mountain of plastic bottles is growing ever higher. Tap water is perfectly safe on Zákynthos, although it is extremely hard. If you carry your own canteen or water bottle, cafés and restaurants you visit will be happy to (re-)fill it for you. Better still, find one of the island's well-regarded springs, from which locals often take their own drinking water.

Greece has delicious bottled fizzy lemonade (*lemonáda*), which, unlike some other 'lemon drinks', does actually contain lemon juice; the best brands are Epsa and Loux. Numerous beer labels are produced in Greece, including by local microbreweries as well as imports. Foreign brands made under licence include Amstel,

LOCAL SPECIALITIES TO TAKE HOME

There are a few Zakynthian specialities which bear testimony to its history of foreign occupation. There is a strong tradition of home jam-making (known as *marmeláda*, from the English 'marmalade'), although you will be lucky to find any outside of private homes. In shops you can also get the very sweet nougat called *mandoláto*, made from almonds and honey, while by the roadside you may see thyme honey (*thymarísio méli*) sold in large jars. If possible, sample from the same batch before buying. Getting stuck with a jar of bogus thyme honey is a risk; the strong, aromatic odour of the real deal, wafting from the container, is unmistakeable.

Zákynthos has its very own premium organic dairy, Basta (tel: 26950 48600), which makes five types of cheese from varying blends of sheep and goat milk. They are open daily 9am–7pm, and you may taste before buying. Find this dairy on the road between the villages of Ágios Léon and Loúha, in the west of the island.

Kaiser and Fischer; nationwide Greek labels are Fix, Mammos (considered to be the best mainstream beers), Nymfi, Alfa, Mythos, and Vergina (especially its red, high-alcohol lager). Zákynthos has its own microbrewery, Levante (www.levantebeer.com), making a bock, pale plus dark lagers, and a wheat beer. You can visit the microbrewery, near Xyngiá beach, and find their products at better local tavernas and shops.

Greece has been making wine for millennia and, although in the past some of its wines have been particularly esteemed, few are now well known outside the country owing to small annual production. Many wineries struggle to exceed 10,000 bottles a year. Zákynthos has a few good local wines and several indigenous or successfully introduced grape cultivars: these include the reds *Katsakoúlias* and *Avgoustiatis*, plus the whites Skiadhopoúlo,

Midgháli and Pávlos. Failing those, mainland labels to watch for in tavernas and shops include three top-drawer, medium-priced reds (Ktima Papaïoannou, Tsantali Rapsani and almost anything from Nemea). For a premium white, try Gentilini Robola from Kefaloniá; Spyropoulos, Tselepos and Skoura vintners from the Peloponnese, and the two Lazaridi wineries from Dhráma, Macedonia. Rosé wine from Amýndeo and surroundings, in western Macedonia, is also reliably quaffable.

Barrelled (*hýma*) wines, usually but not always local, can be surprisingly good, or almost undrinkable; if you're unsure, ask to sample it before committing to a large measure. Resinated wine *(retsína)* can also be good, particularly when served very cold with oily food.

Spirits (Potá)

Anise-flavoured *oúzo* is taken as an aperitif with ice and water; a compound in the anise flavouring makes the mix turn harmlessly cloudy. The most popular brands (like Mini, Varvagianni and Plomari) come from Lésvos Island, though on Zákynthos you may well find Pilavas label from Pátra on the nearby mainland. They all come in sealed 200ml *karafákia* (mini-bottles meant for two diners). *Tsípouro* is a mainland variant of this grape-mash distillate, best without anise, similar to Italian *grappa*. The best, most common mass-market label is Apostolaki from Thessaly; you may also be offered *hýma tsípouro* in measures of up to 500ml. All such spirits are typically served with a small ice bucket; place cubes in your glass, then pour the *oúzo* or *tsípouro* on top, adding water as needed. In summer the ice quickly melts, so don't overdilute it or you will just end up with something akin to soda pop!

Non-alcoholic drinks

Hot coffee (*kafés*) comes as *ellínikós* (generic Middle Eastern or Turkish style, renamed 'Greek' in a patriotic fit after the various

Cyprus crises), freshly brewed in small copper pots (*bríkia*) and served in small cups. It will probably arrive *glykós* (sweet) unless you order *métrios* (medium) or *skétos* (without sugar); extra sweet is *varýglyko*. These are always accompanied by a glass of chilled water. Don't drink to the bottom as that's where the grounds settle; a *kafetzoú* (an older Greek woman skilled in this art) can tell your fortune from the patterns left in the sediment.

Instant coffee is generically known as *nes* or *néskafe*, irrespective of brand; it's pretty unpalatable and headache-inducing, an extra-strength formula for Mediterranean tastes. Since the millennium there has been a backlash against it, so in large resorts and Zákynthos Town you can easily find brewed coffee (*gallikós* or *fíltro*), as well as good cappuccino and espresso. *Fredduccino* – cold cappuccino – is also seasonally popular. Any milky coffee

(though never with *ellinikós*) is *me gála*. *Frappés*, cold instant coffee whipped up in a blender with sugar, ice chips and milk, is refreshing in hot weather.

Soft drinks come in all the international varieties, while Greek-bottled juices are most likely out of cardboard cartons. Bottled (*enfialoméno*) still mineral water is typically from Crete or the Greek mainland mountains. Souroti, Loux and Epsa are the most common domestic sparkling brands. Tuborg is a common soda water brand.

Local wine

TO HELP YOU ORDER…AND PAY

Hello **Hérete/Yiásas**
Good morning **Kaliméra**
Good evening **Kalispéra**
Goodnight **Kaliníkhta**
Goodbye **Adío**
Yes **Ne**
No **Óhi**
Please **Parakaló**
Thank you (very much) **Efharistó (polý)**
Sorry/excuse me **Sygnómi**
Is there a table available, please? **Ypárhi éna diathésimo trapézi, parakaló?**
The menu, please **To katálogos, parakaló**
Could we reserve a table for tonight? **Boroúme na klísoume éna trapézi yia apópse?**
May we order, please? **Na parangiloúme, parakaló?**
I'd like a/some… **Tha íthela éna, mía/meriká…**
I'm a vegetarian **Íme hortofágos**
I'm a vegan **Móno tró nistísima piáta; Íme végan**
I have an allergy to… **Ého allergía se…**
Cheers (as a toast) **Yiámas**
A litre/a half litre (of bulk wine or tsípouro) **Éna kiló/misó kilo**
Enjoy the rest of your meal (literally, 'Good continuation'). **Kalí synnéhia.**
The bill, please. **To logariazmó, parakaló.**

FOOD SHOPS, RESTAURANTS AND BARS

Bar **Baráki**
Old-style restaurant mainly featuring baked dishes **Estiatório/Inomayirío**
Out-of-town restaurant **Exohikó kéndro**

Bakery **Foúrnos**
Café specialising in dairy products **Galaktopolío**
Restaurant specialising in *mezédhes* **Mezedhopolío**
Restaurant specialising in *ouzo* and *mezédhes* **Ouzerí**
Restaurant specialising in tripe soup **Patsatzídhiko**
Specialist fish taverna **Psarotavérna**
Grill house **Psistariá**
Souvláki shop **Souvlatzídhiko**
Restaurant specialising in *tsípouro* and *mezédhes*
    Tsipourádhiko
Patisserie, confectionary shop **Zaharoplastío**

BASIC CONDIMENTS, FOODS, UTENSILS

oil **ládhi**
glass **potíri**
plate **piáto**
cutlery **maheropírouna**
bread (whole meal) **psomí**
    (olikís aléseos)
butter **voútyro**
sugar (brown) **záhari**
    (kastaní)
salt **aláti**
pepper **pipéri**

napkins **hartopetsétes**
eggs **avgá**
yoghurt **yiaoúrti**
onions **kremmýdhia**
pasta (noodles) **makarónia**
honey **méli**
black pepper **mávro pipéri**
rice **rýzi**
lemon **lemóni**
butter **voútyro**
vinegar **xýdi**

... AND READ THE MENU (KATÁLOGOS)

fried **tiganitó**
baked **sto foúrno**
roasted **psitó**
spit-roasted **soúvlas**
grilled **sta kárvouna**
steamed **akhnistó**

stuffed **yemistá**
garlic-flavoured **skórdháto**
red sauce for vegetables
    yiahní
cheese-based red sauce; also
    fried cheese **saganáki**

MEZÉDHES, OREKTIKÁ

marinated small (pizza-topping-size) anchovies **antzoúyies**

fried large anchovies **gávros**

stuffed squash blossoms **kolokythóanthi**

stuffed vine-leaves **dolmádhes**

olives **eliés**

cheese **tyrí**

fried croquettes of courgettes/zucchini **kolokythokeftédhes**

chickpea fritters (like falafel) **revythokeftédhes**

fried small courgettes **kolokythákia tiganitá**

fried aubergine slices **melitzánes tiganités**

fried cheese **saganáki**

mushroom pie **manitarópita**

spinach pie (in a taverna, usually baked, a big portion) **spanakópita**

grey mullet- or cod-roe dip **taramosaláta**

cheese pies, small **tyropitákia**

yoghurt dip with garlic and cucumber **tzatziki**

yellow split-pea mash **fáva**

MEAT

Meat, any **kréas**

sausages **loukánika**

small fried meatballs **keftedhákia**

beef, veal **moskhári**

pork **hirinó**

chicken **kotópoulo**

veal/beef **moskhári**

lamb **arní**

goat, kid **katsíki, katsikáki**

rabbit **kounéli**

mince 'hamburger' **biftéki**

pork chop **brizóla**

veal chop **spalobrizóla**

meatballs baked in red sauce **soutzoukákia**

FISH (PSÁRI) AND SEAFOOD (THALASSINÁ)

fresh **frésko**

frozen **katapsygméno**

brine-cured **pastó(s)**

cured bonito slices **lakérdha**

small shrimp (often in sauce) **garidhákia**

bigger grilling shrimp **garídhes**

octopus **okhtapódi**
red mullet **barboúni**
goatfish (small red mullet)
    koutsomoúra
swordfish **xifías**
fresh hake **bakalarákia**
picarel **marídhes**

sandsmelt, silverside **atherína**
baby squid **kalamarákia,
    gónos**
mussels **mýdhia**
sardines **sardhéles**
cuttlefish **soupiá**

VEGETABLES

salad, any **saláta**
'Greek' salad **horiátiki saláta**
lettuce maroúli
green onion **frésko
    kremmýdhi**
dill **ánitho**
cabbage-carrot salad
    láhano-karóto
tomatoes **domátes**
olives **eliés**
boiled greens **hórta**
runner/string beans
    ambelofásola
artichokes (stewed hearts)
    angináres (ala políta)
peas **arakádhes**

stuffed tomatoes **domátes
    yemistés**
baked stuffed bell peppers
    piperiés yemistés
cheese-stuffed fried
    long peppers **piperies
    yemistés me tyrí**
aubergine/eggplant
    melitzána
chickpeas **revýthia**
potatoes, fried **patátes
    tiganités**
blonde haricot beans **fasólia
    yígandes**
courgettes, zucchini (boiled)
    kolokythákia

FRUITS

orange **portokáli**
grapes **stafýlia**
figs **sýka**
watermelon **karpoúzi**
apricots **verýkoka**

Persian melon **pepóni**
big pears **akhládhi**
miniature pears **krystália**
figs **sýka**
apple **mílo**

WHERE TO EAT

The following prices reflect the average cost of a two-course meal (per person) plus a half litre of hýma wine. At all restaurants an automatic tax of 13 percent (VAT) is always included in the menu-listed prices of food and non-alcoholic drinks; all booze, whether beer, wine or stronger spirits, is taxed at 24%. If service has been good, it is customary to leave an additional five to 10 percent for the waiter, especially if they are an employee and not the owner. Most town restaurants operate year-round but those in the resorts and villages only from May to October, unless otherwise stated.

€€€€	over €45
€€€	€35–45
€€	€22–35
€	less than €22

ZÁKYNTHOS TOWN

Akrotíri Taverna €€ *Akrotíri, 4km (2.5 miles) north of Zákynthos Town centre, tel: 26950 45712*. A pleasant summer-only taverna with a large garden. Grilled meats are a speciality but staff also bring round large trays of tempting *mezédhes* from which you pick and choose. Prices are reasonable, and the house wine is more than acceptable.

Bastouni Tou Agiou € *Underneath the Port Authority premises at the landward end of the ferry quay, tel: 26950 24045*. Café cum restaurant that does decent English and other breakfasts plus a range of snacks, including beetroot salad and seafood platters. Occasional informal music sessions.

Komis €€€ *Bastoúni tou Agíou, tel: 26950 26915*. A lovely psarotavérna tucked into a rather unlikely spot behind the port authority building (opposite Ágios Dhionýsios cathedral). The emphasis is on fresh and inventive fish and seafood dishes (think sea urchins and clams), but it does come with a hefty price tag. There is a good list of *mezédhes*, good wine and, better still, some really rather tempting desserts.

Malanos € *Agíou Athanasíou 38, Kípi district (south of the river off Kalamáki road), tel: 26950 45936.* A deservedly popular and inexpensive all-year shrine of *mayireftá* (already cooked dishes); mince-rich *youvarlákia* and *fasolákia yahní* are typical offerings. There's also unusually good bread as well as the expected barrel wine. Often hosts live *kandádes* at weekends. Sociable vibe and welcoming staff.

Prosilio €€€ *Agíon Pándon and A. Latta 15, tel: 26950 22040,* www.prosili-ozakynthos.gr. Located next to central Platía Solomoú, this stylish modern restaurant serves traditional Greek fare with a creative twist – for example lamb with Jerusalem artichokes and goat's cheese – and a selection of fine wines. Its lovely garden is an additional attraction; ask for an outdoor table in the summer

Stathmos €€ *Filitá 42, tel: 26950 24040.* The former bus station, just a block behind the seafront, has surprisingly become a delightful old-style *inomayirío* (wine-and-cookshop), serving a fine selection of *mezédhes* such as *saganáki* preceding seafood or meaty main courses.

Varkarola € *Lomvárdhou 30, corner Xénou, tel: 26950 26999,* http://varkarola. gr. Attractively designed establishment that offers traditional home-made dishes such as rosemary rabbit and pork shank, plus good lunchtime deals. The best place in town to come for nightly *kantádhes*, featuring vocal trio, mandolin and guitar.

VASILIKÓS AND LAGANÁS BAY

Agnandi Taverna €€ *At Xirokástello beyond Argási, 8km (5 miles) from Zákynthos Town, tel: 26950 35183.* An modern wooden building on a steep slope overlooking the sea. Slightly touristy, but the homestyle recipes are authentic and tasty. The menu covers the generic standards, but also has interesting daily/seasonal specials.

Apelati € *1km (0.6 miles) north of inland Kerí village, tel: 26950s 43324.* This lovely rural tavern, tucked behind a field off the main road, offers a selection of wholesome country dishes from fresh meat and fish to delicious salads, much of it made from own-grown produce.

Bel Mare €€ *Dháfni beach, tel: 6974 010136*. As you'd expect, fish and seafood are featured here. Nice setting, with a lawn-and-sunbeds out front. Decor includes a massive hat collection on the ceiling.

Café stou Nitzi € *Central platía of inland Kerí village, tel: 26950 43205*. Brilliantly colourful, quirky café on the square that somehow manages to combine a traditional feel with trendy modern sensibilities. For example, there's a glass top table heaped with tiny toys in primary colours. Good coffee, snacks, cakes and ice cream made and served by friendly proprietor Angeliki.

Dennis €€ *Lithákia, tel: 26950 51387*, www.dennistaverna.com. A bit of an institution (since 1976), and open all year round, Dennis is a friendly, family-run taverna with great atmosphere, serving a wide range of traditional food. Try the *mezédhes* and charcoal-grilled meat – the pork chops are legendary; the house wine isn't bad either. There is also free transport back to your villa or hotel should you need it.

To Keri €€ *Límni Kerioú shoreline, tel: 26950 43756*, www.keritaverna.gr. This restaurant specialises in grilled meat, such as very tender liver, fish and lobster-spaghetti. Lots of salads and dips, of which the *tzatzíki* is exceptional.

Kerí Lighthouse Restaurant €€€ *Kerí village, tel: 26950 43384*. The taverna nearest the lighthouse is well worth a visit, even if you just plan on ordering a drink and gazing at the Kerí Caves from above and admiring the sea views. The food is enjoyable if overpriced – but after all, what you are really paying for is the view.

To Spitiko €€ *Límni Kerioú seafront, tel: 26950 49198*. Great range of all-time favourites doled out in big portions, and a few dishes not often found elsewhere, for example *moskhári tis stámnas* (beef cooked in a clay vessel). *Mezédhes* include exceptional *kolokythokeftédhes*. Lovely aromatic *hýma* white wine.

Sarakina € *2km (1.2 miles) west of Laganás, tel: 26950 51606*. Occupying a rambling old house with outdoor terraces amidst the olive groves, this evening-only taverna offers a huge range of quality local food and wine, as well as traditional music, popular with Greeks and tourists alike. It is well advertised in Laganás, and a free, frequent and rather handy minibus shuttles diners between town and the restaurant.

Theodoritsis €€ *Just past Argási towards Vasilikós village, tel: 26950 48500.* Theodoritsis is where the beau monde of Zákynthos go for a weekend blow-out; the stress is on *magireftá*, but grills and *mezédhes* are also available. Moderately pricy. Summer terrace overlooking town and tasteful interior. Open all year.

To Triodi €€ *Gérakas, tel: 26950 35215.* Lovely garden taverna next door to the Turtle Information Centre, where you can enjoy a variety of filling meat and fish dishes, vegetarian platters or smaller salads and snacks before or after a dip at the fantastic beach here. There's live Greek music on most evenings.

Zakanthl €€ *Kalamáki, tel: 26950 43586,* www.facebook.com/zakanthi. This is probably the most attractive place to dine or drink (it styles itself as a 'lounge bar') in Kalamáki, with seating In a large well-maintained garden with subdued lighting after sunset; some nights there is live jazz. The quite decent food mixes simple staples like pasta, pizza with more typical Greek offerings (grills and salads).

THE WEST AND NORTH

Amboula € *Tragáki shore annexe, tel: 26950 65085.* An all-rounder taverna with great sea views, purveying a mix of Greek and generic Mediterranean cuisine, strong on seafood.

Asian Feast € *Plános, tel: 6946 828614.* One of this resort's prime restaurants serves both Indian and Chinese cuisine, with dishes such as peshwari naan, onion bhajis, chicken vindaloo, biryani, lamb tikka and Peking duck. Portions are sizeable and serving staff are charming.

Cross (Stavrós) €€ *Kambí, tel: 26950 48481 or 697 3334560.* A family-owned taverna with an unbeatable location and amazing sea views, especially in the evening. Freshly cooked traditional local fare at reasonable prices. Live Greek music on some days.

Kaki Rahi €€ *Pigadhákia, near the Vertzagio Folklore Museum, tel: 26950 83580.* This restaurant offers a decent range of *magireftá*, grills and *mezédhes*, served on a charming leafy terrace beside a running stream. Excellent bulk wine (note the old barrels inside) on offer also; accessible by day using the *trenáki* from Alykés.

Mikro Nisi €€ *Eponymous cove 1km (0.6 miles) beyond Makrýs Gialós, tel: 6973 050680.* Good value generic taverna fare – *horiátiki*, *kalamarákia*, *souvláki* and the like – served in a delightful setting. The taverna is perched on the edge of a small headland (the 'Small Island' of the name) overlooking a tiny harbour and you watch the boats come and go as you eat. A tranquil spot for languid lunches and dinners.

To Paradosiako €€ *Alykés, tel: 26950 83412,* https://paradosiako.com.gr. On the main road coming in from the south, this restaurant lives up to its name, meaning "traditional", by appealing to locals. It has unusual dishes like swordfish in tarragon sauce, and a well-selected wine list. A little off the beaten path, but well worth the effort.

Pilarinos € *Makrýs Gialós, tel: 26950 31396.* Set on a slight hill just above this small but pleasant beach, this summer-only taverna offers a tasty range of grilled meat and fish, plus plenty of salads and dips. Lovely place for light lunches post-swim.

Porto Limnionas €€ *Pórto Limniónas, near Ágios Léon, tel: 26957 72072.* Location can count for a lot, and this restaurant has one of the best on the island. The food is reasonably priced, standard taverna fare, plus some less common *mezédhes* and pricier fish dishes, all served on a promontory overlooking an idyllic rocky bay. To cap things off, the restaurant faces west, so is a great place to watch the sun set.

Porto Roulis €€ *Kypséli Beach, near Dhrosiá, tel: 26950 61628.* A friendly place, popular with islanders, overlooking the sea and a narrow beach, this gets very fresh fish (one of its main attractions) but also has a good line in the usual Greek salads and vegetables. The house wine is drinkable, and the freshness of all the ingredients make a trip here well worth the short detour off the main road.

TRAVEL ESSENTIALS

PRACTICAL INFORMATION

A

ACCESSIBLE TRAVEL

In general travellers with disabilities are not well catered for in Greece, though, as relevant EU-wide legislation is implemented, things are gradually improving. Wheelchair ramps and beeps for the sight-impaired are rare at pedestrian crossings, and few buses are accessible for those with mobility needs.

Zákynthos beach resorts and the centre of the main town are fairly flat, so wheelchair users should not encounter major problems when out and about there. Specific hotels are a different matter; since 2018, all new-built premises must by law include at least two rooms with an accessible bathroom; older lodgings may have been retrofitted, but this cannot be relied upon. Do make any accessibility needs clear at the point of booking, whether booking directly with an establishment or via a package-holiday operator.

One new development at many Greek beaches is a ramp for wheelchair-users access swimmable deep water.

ACCOMMODATION

Hotels. Many hotels are heavily booked with package tours in summer, especially between early July and early September, so reservations are strongly recommended at these times. Recourse to the usual third-party booking websites can be successful; in slow years package operators have online specials, or you could try Zakynthos Villas (https://www.zakynthos-villas.com, tel: 2695024624), the website of local villa owners. However, be aware that by booking though Greek websites, you forego any of the legal/financial protections afforded by using a UK-based and -bonded ABTA member.

Villas and apartments. There are many villas, apartments and studios (the latter terms are interchangeable) in Zákynthos available to rent. Accommodation ranges from simple rooms to lavishly appointed summer homes – sometimes tastefully converted from a traditional house or houses – complete with a swimming pool.

In the UK, companies offering top-of-the-range secluded luxury villas on

Zákynthos include:

James Villa Holidays tel: 0800 074 0122, www.jamesvillas.co.uk/destinations/the-greek-islands/zakynthos

Simpon Travel tel: 020 8392 5858, https://www.simpsontravel.com/villas-zakynthos

SJ Villas tel: 020 7351 684, https://sjvillas.co.uk/greece/zakynthos

The Villa Collection tel: 020 7183 3554, https://thevillacollection.com/greece/zakynthos

> I'd like a single/double room/family apartment **Tha íthela éna monóklino/díklino domátio/ikoyeniakó dhiamérizma**
> What's the rate per night? **Póso stihízi yia káthe vrádhi?**

AIRPORTS

Located 4km (3 miles) southwest of Zákynthos Town at Gaïtáni, this busy airport was thoroughly overhauled by German operator Fraport between 2017 and 2019. If you have booked your holiday through a UK tour operator you will be met at the airport and whisked off in a coach to your villa or resort, otherwise you will have to take a taxi to wherever you are staying (consult https://www.zantetaxi.gr/rates/ for an idea of what you will pay), or coincide with one of the four daily Mon–Sat services between here and the town KTEL terminal. Zákynthos is connected domestically by air to Athens (4–5 daily, 1hr); Corfu (summer 3 weekly, 2hr); Kefaloniá (summer 3 weekly, 25min); Préveza (summer 3 weekly, 75min). For a comprehensive table of today's flight arrivals and departures, consult www.greek-airports.gr/zakinth.html.

B

BICYCLE AND MOTORCYCLE HIRE

You can hire bicycles, motorcycles and quad bikes in all the tourist centres.

However, many package operators warn clients against motorised cycles and scooters for the quite legitimate fear of an accident (and to drum up more business for their organised excursions). It is vital that you check that motorbike hire does not invalidate your holiday insurance. Scooter hire is cheap (you should be quoted a rate per day, including third-party insurance and CDW collision-damage waiver). To hire a motorbike with an engine of 50–90cc displacement you must be at least 18 years old and hold a driving license authorised for Class AM (look on the back of a UK one). USA licenses must include Class M. Rental agencies have become quite strict on this point – zealous police are fining both them and riders up to €1,000 for contraventions. If you don't possess the appropriate license, which must be carried with you as you drive, agencies will push you to hire a quad bike; however these are notoriously unstable, and crash helmets will be pointedly provided. It is in fact illegal to ride two-wheeled scooters without a crash helmet – the fines issued at checkpoints are similarly draconian, payable at a major post office.

It is inadvisable to ride a motorbike in shorts or a swimsuit, since burns or scrapes resulting from even a slight accident could be appalling; clinics and hospital casualty wards are wearily familiar with treating 'road rash'. Test brakes, lights and tyres before hiring, and drive with care. Even on good roads there are occasional potholes or treacherous stretches of loose gravel.

Bicycle hire is somewhat less common, but quite feasible for the flatter parts of Zákynthos, and jaunts within the same resort. See page 66 for a recommended outlet in Zákynthos Town.

BUDGETING FOR YOUR TRIP

Zákynthos is not the cheapest of the Greek islands, and these days probably as costly as most other Mediterranean destinations. In high season, the rate for a good 4-star hotel is around €200 minimum per night for a double room. Booking an airfare/accommodation package will yield substantial savings. Otherwise, independent travellers can find return flights for under £100–200, decent places to stay from around €60–70 per night for a double room, with big discounts available outside of peak summer season.

Eating out is considerably cheaper if you stick to *magireftá* and simple grills and *mezédhes* in places also frequented by locals: generally a three-course meal plus drinks in a decent restaurant or taverna will cost around €15–25 per person, assuming two or more adult diners. Public transport and museum fees are inexpensive.

C

CAR HIRE

Unless visiting the island with the intention of walking or cycling, you might consider hiring a car on Zákynthos, where the bus service is very patchy. As elsewhere in Greece, car hire is not particularly cheap, but it is certainly less expensive than touring by taxi. Car hire starts from about €30 per day in low season (with a €500–750 excess on insurance for damage). For a decent family-sized car in high season, you should budget at least €300 per week; all have air conditioning these days.

Better third-party consolidator websites include www.auto-europe.co.uk, www.carrentals.co.uk and www.rentalcargroup.com. Post-Brexit, for now UK licenses are also honoured but it's wise to secure an IDP from any major UK post office branch before departure; bring your UK license (minimum age 18), one passport-sized photo and cash for a small (currently £5.50) fee – they should be issued on the spot.

You'll find car-hire firms across Zákynthos, at least in tourist resorts. To be on the safe side, reserve a car ahead of time, especially for the high season. Local firms generally charge slightly less than international agencies and provide equally good cars and service. International chains that operate here, bookable through their websites, include Avis, Budget, Europcar, Hertz, National, Sixt and Thrifty.

Many brochure rates seem attractive because they do not include personal insurance, collision damage waiver (CDW) or VAT at 24 percent. Most agencies have a waiver excess of between €400 and €750 – the amount (pre-blocked on your credit card) you're responsible for if your vehicle gets smashed or stolen, even with CDW coverage. It is strongly suggested you purchase extra cover (often called Super CDW or Liability Waiver Surcharge) to reduce this risk to zero; UK or North American residents can buy good-value annual policies from entities like Insurance4CarHire (www.insurance4carhire.com) or iCar Hire Insurance (www.icarhireinsurance.com). Policies sold on the spot are invariably rip-offs.

You will almost always need a credit card for the deposit (though you may pay the actual rental charge with a debit card) and a full national licence (held for at least one year) from your country of residence. If you are from a non-EU country, it is also mandatory to have an international driving permit – another little-known law which is increasingly enforced. Depending on the model and the hire company, the minimum age for hiring a car varies from 21 to 25. Third-party liability insurance (CDW) is usually included in the stated rate, but with an excess amount that can be up to €800, so it is always worth paying a little more for comprehensive coverage, particularly a policy that insures you for a crash with a third party.

What's the hire charge for a full day? **Póso kostízi giá mía méra?**
I'd like to hire a car (tomorrow) **Tha íthela na nikiáso éna
    aftokínito (ávrio)**

CLIMATE

July and August are the sunniest, hottest and busiest tourist months. You may prefer to visit between mid-May and late June or from early September to mid-October. It can rain at any time of year, though showers are much less likely in July and August. The Ionians are the greenest of all the Greek island chains, because in winter it rains very hard. November and December are the wettest months and January the coldest, but even during mid-winter the climate is moderate, with hard freezes very rare. Spring, when the island bursts with wildflowers, is the best time for walking or cycling in the countryside.

The chart below shows each month's average air and sea temperature in Celsius and Fahrenheit, and the average number of hours of sunshine per day.

	J	F	M	A	M	J	J	A	S	O	N	D
Air												
°C	11	11	12	15	20	24	27	27	23	20	16	12
°F	52	52	54	60	68	75	80	81	74	67	60	54
Sea												
°C	16	15	15	16	19	23	25	27	26	23	20	18
°F	61	59	59	61	66	72	77	79	78	73	68	64
Sunshine hours												
	4	5	6	8	10	11	12	12	10	7	5	4

CLOTHING

Clothing is invariably casual on the islands. However, the Greeks do like to dress up when they go out in the evening and visitors who make a bit of an effort will be smiled upon – conversely, beach garb except at lunchtime by the sea is frowned on. With regard to comfort, choose lightweight cotton clothing in spring and summer, and a warm jacket, sweater and rainwear in autumn and winter – waterproof gear is also useful for seagoing excursions. Since it rains from time to time, outside of July and August, a protective coat or umbrella might be a good idea. Plastic shoes or 'trekking' sandals are extremely useful for stony beaches; these are available from beach-side tourist shops.

CRIME AND SAFETY (SEE ALSO EMERGENCIES)

The Zakynthians are, like the vast majority of Greek people, scrupulously honest. However, thefts do unfortunately occur, so it's sensible to leave valuables in the hotel safe. Look after your passport but at the same time be aware that you're required to have official ID on your person at all times in Greece; a photocopy should suffice for beach outings.

Possession of drugs is a very serious matter in Greece, carrying a stiff mandatory sentence and potentially long spells being held on remand. Make sure you have a prescription from your doctor if you will be carrying syringes, insulin, any narcotic drugs or even codeine, which is illegal in Greece, though recent luggage searches for the popular USA compound empirin-codeine are essentially unknown. Interestingly, cannabis supplements containing CBD are legal here (Cannaboss is a major producer; www.cannaboss.gr) and can be bought at certain shops. Spliffs, though, are another matter entirely.

D

DRIVING

Road conditions. Zákynthos has a deserved reputation for having some of the most dangerous roads in Greece, so be very careful. The surfaces on main roads are generally very good, though curves in the road are often indicated too late, are sometimes unsignposted and are never banked correctly. If there is a mirror on a bend, downshift; it is probably going to be extremely tight or narrow, or perhaps both, with or without oncoming traffic.

On clifftop roads it is very dangerous to pass, so be patient if there is a slow-moving bus or heavy vehicle in front of you. Conversely, try to let local speed demons pass you as soon as it is safe to do so.

Zákynthos secondary roads are some of the narrowest on any of the Greek islands – it's difficult to safely exceed 50kph (31mph) – while anything marked 'unsurfaced' on a map can be very rough indeed. Rockslides are common during or just after the rainy season, and broken-up verges/shoulders or potholes are not unknown on even the best-paved stretches. Drive with extreme caution, as you might be held responsible for damage sustained to the underside or windshield of your hire car, even with comprehensive coverage.

Are we on the right road for…? **Páme kalá yia…?**
Fill the tank please, with (low-test, 95 octane) petrol **Parakaló, gemíste tin me enenindapendári**
My car has broken down **To avtokínito mou éhi páthi vlávi**
There's been an accident **Égine éna atýhima**

Driving regulations. Drive on the right side and pass on the left. Traffic from the right has right of way. A Greek practice to be aware of is that if a driver flashes the lights, it usually means 'Stay where you are, I'm coming through', not 'Go ahead'. (Occasionally it may mean 'Beware, traffic police control ahead!') Seat belts are obligatory, as is the carrying of your driving licence while at the wheel; there is a €200 fine if you are caught without it. The speed limit is 50kph (31mph) inside built-up areas (Zákynthos Town and all resorts), 80kph (50mph) in the countryside. In practice, however, rural road conditions set their own speed limit.

Other drivers constitute a major hazard. Greeks love to straddle the median line, barge out recklessly from side-roads, or overtake on either side. One-way street systems are often regarded, especially by two-wheeled drivers, as optional.

Fuel. Generally speaking, you will never be far from a filling station, though in parts of the north and west of Zákynthos they are few and far between. Note that in rural areas filling stations are open only until about 8pm, and most close on Sunday. On busy main roads and in resorts they open daily from early until late. A few big filling stations have after-hours automatic-sales pumps, using debit/credit cards or euro notes.

If you need help. Your car hire office should provide contact numbers for breakdown service. If you are involved in an accident with another vehicle and/or with significant personal injury or property damage, it is illegal to leave

---

Detour **Παράκαμψη/Parákampsi**
Parking **Παρκιγκ/Párking**
No parking **Απαγορεύεται/Apagorévete to párking**
Be careful **Προσοχή/Prosohí**
Bus stop **Στάση λεοφορείου/Stási leoforíou**
For pedestrians **Για πεζούς/Yia pezoús**
Danger, dangerous **Κίνδυνος, επικίνδυνος/Kíndynos, epikíndhynos**
Entry forbidden **Απαγορεύεται η είσοδος/Apagorévete i ísodhos**

the scene – wait for the ordinary police or traffic police *(trohéa)* to show up and take statements.

Road signs. On main roads and at junctions these will be in Greek and Latin (Western) letters; on secondary roads they may just be in Greek (for some important ones see the list). Critical junctions are atrociously indicated, with vital signs sometimes either uprooted or hidden by foliage.

E

ELECTRICITY

Greece has 220-volt/50-cycle AC current out of European Type F (earthed, heavy-duty apparatus) or Type C (unearthed) two-pin sockets, so bring an adapter or transformer with you as necessary (though plug adaptors can be found at better-stocked electrical goods merchants).

a transformer **énas metashimatistís**
an adapter **énas prosarmostís**

EMBASSIES AND CONSULATES

British Honorary Vice Consulate: Foskólou 28, Zákynthos Town; tel: 26950 22906 (calls will be automatically forwarded to the main consulate in Athens). For serious emergencies, just go to the premises from 9am–2pm working days.

Embassies *(presvíes)* or full consulates *(proxenía)* of all major countries are located in Athens.

Australian Embassy: Hatziyianni Mexi 5, Level 2, by the Hilton Hotel, 115 28 Athens, https://greece.embassy.gov.au

British Embassy: Ploutárhou 1, 106 75 Athens, tel: 210 72 72 600, www.gov.uk/world/organisations/british-embassy-athens

Canadian Embassy: Ethnikís Andistáseos 48, Halándri, 152 31 Athens, tel:

210 72 73 400, www.canadainternational.gc.ca/greece-grece
Irish Embassy Vassiléos Konstandínou 7, 106 74 Athens, tel: 210 72 32 771/2, www.dfa.ie/embassies/irish-embassies-abroad/europe/greece/
South African Embassy and Consulate: Kifisías 60, 151 25 Maroúsi, Athens, tel: 210 6179 020
US Embassy and Consulate: Vassilísis Sofías 91, 101 60 Athens, tel: 210 72 12 951, https://gr.usembassy.gov

EMERGENCIES
Police: (all-purpose emergency number) **100**; (Zákynthos Town) tel: 26950 22100.
Tourist Police: (Zákynthos Town) Lomvárdhou 62, tel: 26951 24483.
Hospitals: (Zákynthos Town) tel: 26950 59100.
Ambulance: 166; (Zákynthos Town) tel: 26950 23166.
Fire Reporting: 199.
Port Authority: (Zákynthos Town) tel: 26950 28118.

G

GETTING AROUND
The local bus consortium (KTEL, https://ktel-zakynthos.gr/en/routes) has a list of local routes and frequencies, which tend be fairly sparse.

GETTING THERE
It is possible to cross Europe overland and take the ferry from Italy to Pátra on the Greek mainland and then from Kyllíni, further down the coast, to Zákynthos Town. From the UK you can fly directly into Zákynthos on easyJet, www.easyjet.com or British Airways (www.ba.com) from May to early October – if you choose not to use the charter flight provided by package operators. Out of season, you will have to fly to Athens first, from where there are daily domestic flights on Olympic (www.olympicair.com), or Sky Express (www.skyexpress.gr) to Zákynthos (45 minutes), or take the coach from the Kifissoú bus station (several daily to Zákynthos, around 7 hours; all coaches connect with

ferries for which there is a small additional cost).

H

HEALTH AND MEDICAL CARE

In theory, UK citizens with a Global Health Insurance Card (obtainable free online at www.nhs.uk/using-the-nhs/healthcare-abroad/apply-for-a-free-uk-global-health-insurance-card-ghic/) can get free treatment under the Greek health service. However, you are likely to receive the minimum treatment; medication must be paid for (the prescription itself from the state doctor should be fee-free) and state hospital facilities are over-stretched in the tourist season. It's therefore preferable to obtain private medical insurance for your holiday. Doctors and dentists are concentrated in Zákynthos Town; your hotel or apartment owner will be able to find you one who speaks English. Most resorts have a local, private medical clinic.

Hospital. The hospital on Zákynthos (https://zante-hospital.gr/en/) is found 4km west of town at Gaïtáni, operating a 24-hour emergency service; their website also has a list of duty pharmacies.

Pharmacies. A green cross on a white background identifies a pharmacy (ΦΑΡΜΑΚΕΙΟ – *farmakío*). They are normally open only during the morning Monday to Friday but a notice on the door should tell you the nearest one for after-hours service. One pharmacy is always open in Zákynthos Town at night and on Saturday and Sunday. Without a prescription, you can't get sleeping pills, antibiotics, barbiturates or certain medicines for stomach upsets.

While swimming near rocks, look out for sea urchins – their black spines

a doctor/dentist **énas yiatrós/odontoíatros**
hospital **nosokomío**
indigestion **varystomahiá**
sunstroke **ilíasi**
a fever **pyretós**

are very sharp and will break off in your skin. If this happens, seek medical attention, as they are very tricky to remove, but need to be; left unattended, the entry point and area below festers, since the hollow spines act as ideal conduits for microbes.

L

LANGUAGE

Only in remote countryside spots will non-Greek-speaking tourists run into serious communication problems. You will find that basic English is spoken almost everywhere, as are other languages such as Italian, German and French, to some degree.

Stress is a very important feature of the Greek language, denoted by an accent above the vowel of the syllable to be emphasised. We have indicated proper stress in all of our transliterations of multi-syllable words

The table given below lists the Greek letters in their upper- and lower-case forms, followed by the closest individual or combined letters to which they correspond in the English language, and a pronunciation guide. Do not

Double letters

ΑΙ αι	ey	as in *they*
ΑΥ	αυ αv	as in *avant-garde*
ΕΙ ει	i	as in *ski*
ΓΚ γκ		*Hard g when initial, 'ng' when medial*
ΟΥ	ου ou	as in *soup*
ΓΓ γγ	ng	as in *longer; always medial*
ΓΞ γξ	nx	as in *anxious; always medial*
ΜΠ	μπ	*b if initial, mb when medial*
ΝΤ	ντ	*d if initial, nd when medial*

be alarmed if you encounter other transliterations on Zákynthos – several schemes exist. For example, the word *ágios* is often also spelled *ághios* and *áyios* in the Roman alphabet, although it is always pronounced the same all over the island.

Α α	a	as in **fa**ther
Β β	v	as in **v**eto
Γ γ	y	as in **g**o (except pronounced 'y' before 'e' and 'i' sounds, when it's like the y in **y**es)
Δ δ	dh	like **th** in then
Ε ε	e	as in **g**et
Ζ ζ	z	as in English
Η η	i	as in **ski**
Θ θ	th	like **th** in thin
Ι ι	i	as in **ski**
Κ κ	k	as in English
Λ λ	l	as in English
Μ μ	m	as in English
Ν ν	n	as in English
Ξ ξ	x	as in exercise
Ο ο	o	as in road
Π π	p	as in English
Ρ ρ	r	as in English but rolled more
Σ σ/ς	s	as in **kiss**, except like z before m or g sounds
Τ τ	t	as in English
Υ υ	y	as in country
Φ φ	f	as in English
Χ χ	h	as in Scottish 'loch'
Ψ ψ	ps	as in ti**ps**y
Ω ω	o	as in **bo**ne

LGBTQ+ TRAVELLERS

Zákynthos has no specific LGBTQ+ scene, but attitudes in resorts are generally relaxed. Unfortunately, travellers may encounter some hostility in conservative rural communities. Homosexuality is legal in Greece for people aged 17 and older.

M

MAPS

The best maps available of Zákynthos are issued by Terrain Editions (http://terrainmaps.gr/#products). Either their 1:50,000 'Zakynthos' no. 305 or the newer 355 is clear and accurate and give place names in both Greek letters and in transliteration. They are available locally at newsagents or tourist shops, or before departure in the UK through through the Map Centre (www.the-mapcentre.com/zakynthos-or-zante-150000-terrain-map-7418-p.asp). Free tourist maps of much inferior quality are widely available, for example from car hire offices.

MEDIA

Newspapers and magazines (efimerídhes; periodhiká). During the tourist season, foreign-language newspapers are on sale at shops and kiosks on the island, generally available the same day. Greek news in English can be found at www.ekathimerini.com and https://greekreporter.com/greek-news/.

Television (tiliórasi). Most hotels and many bars offer satellite television networks, including CNN, BBC World and, in the busier resorts, Sky.

Radio. BBC World Service is no longer broadcast on short wave but can be streamed on www.bbc.co.uk. Note that live sports events will not be broadcast.

MONEY

Currency (nómisma). In common with most other Western European countries, the euro (EUR or €) is the official currency used in Greece. Notes are in denominations of 5, 10, 20, 50, 100 and 200 euros; coins in 1 and 2 euros and

1, 2, 5, 10, 20 and 50 cents, known as *leptá* in Greece. Notes of 100 euros and above are regarded with suspicion, as possibly counterfeit, and can often only be exchanged in banks. 500-euro notes were withdrawn from circulation in 2018 because of their association with crime.

Banks and currency exchange. You'll find banks in Zákynthos Town and in the larger resort areas. Most banks exchange foreign currency notes but charge a commission (usually 1–3 percent) for the service. Exchange rates appear on a digital display, and are identical for each bank. Major hotels and a scant few travel agencies (the latter sometimes called 'tourist offices') are authorised to change money, but you will probably get less for your money than you would from a bank even if the service is advertised as 'commission free'.

ATMs. The easiest method to obtain cash is through 'hole-in-the-wall' cash dispensers. These can be found in Zákynthos Town and in all the larger resorts. Depending upon your own individual card fees, this might also be the cheapest way to get money.

Credit and debit cards. As part of the Greek government's campaign to stamp out the thriving black economy, card transactions are actively encouraged at hotels, tavernas, supermarkets and filling stations. Surprisingly unlikely-looking enterprises have the necessary device, though American Express and Diners Club have very limited acceptance.

Travellers cheques. These are explicitly not recommended for use anywhere in Greece. Expect severe delays or outright refusals in banks; no agency will accept them.

I want to change some pounds/dollars **Thélo na allákso merikés líres/meriká dollária**

Do you have a card (Point of Sale) apparatus? **Éhete syskeví POS?**

O

OPENING TIMES

Mikró ýpno (the Geek early afternoon nap) is still alive and well on Zákynthos, observed and enforced by law most strictly outside tourist areas. Do not disturb people at home between 3 and 6pm; neither should you make any loud noise (music systems, chain saws, revving engines, etc) during that time.

Shops. Traditional hours are generally Mon–Sat 8.30 or 9am–2 or 2.30pm. On Tuesday, Thursday and Friday shops reopen in the evening from 5.30 or 6pm until 8.30–9pm. Shops catering to tourists often stay open all through the day and until late each evening in the summer, as well as part of Sunday. Larger supermarkets open Mon–Fri 8.30am–9pm and Sat 9am–8pm; in resort areas you will find at least one supermarket with Sunday hours (typically 9am–2pm or 10am–4pm).

Museums and tourist attractions. State-run museums are closed on Tuesdays, typically open Wed–Sat 8.30am–3.30pm and Sun 8.30 or 9.30am–2.30 or 3pm. Private museums are less reliable and often must be phoned to book a visit.

Banks. Mon–Fri 8am–2pm.

Businesses and offices. 8am–1pm, then 2–5pm. Government offices work 8am–1.30pm, sometimes 2pm, and don't reopen.

Restaurants and tavernas. More traditional establishments open for lunch from noon until around 3.30pm and for dinner from 7pm to 11.15pm or later.

P

POLICE

The tourist police (*touristikí astynomía*) have a specific mission to help visitors to the island, as well as to accompany state inspectors of hotels and restaurants to ensure that proper standards and prices are maintained.

Traffic police check car documents and driving licences, operate speed traps and issue fines for illegal parking (fines in Greece are high). Car-hire companies will use your credit-card details to pay ignored parking tickets; you have 10 working days to pay moving violations in person. Failing that, a court date will be set, and a summons sent to your home address. Failure to appear will result in an extra conviction for contempt of court, and make future re-entry to Greece potentially difficult.

Emergency telephone number: 100.

Tourist police: tel: 26951 24483.

Where's the nearest police station? **Pou íne to kondinótero astynomikó tmíma?**

POST OFFICES

Post offices (labelled ΕΛΤΑ for Elliniká Tahydhromía) handle letters, parcels and money orders but no longer exchange foreign currency. Look for a blue sign with a stylised head of Hermes traced on it in yellow.

Post offices are generally open Mon–Fri 7.30am–2pm. Registered letters and parcels to non-EU destinations are checked before being sent, so don't seal them until presenting them at the desk. The main post office in Zákynthos Town is at Yeoryíou Tertséti 11a (Mon–Fri 7.30am–4pm), one block inland from the shoreline boulevard.

Letterboxes are yellow but if there are two slots, make sure you use the one marked *exoterikó* (abroad). In tourist hotels, the receptionist will take care of

Have you received any mail for…? **Éhete grámmata giá…?**
a stamp for this letter/postcard **éna grammatósimo giaftó to grámma/giaftí tin kart postál**
express (special delivery) **katepígon**
registered **systiméno**

dispatching your mail. It is best to leave letters at a proper post office, since most letterboxes have infrequent collections.

PUBLIC HOLIDAYS

Banks, offices and shops are closed on the following national holidays, as well as during some feasts and festivals (see also the Calendar of events on page 73):

1 January *Protohroniá* New Year's Day
6 January *Ágia Theofánia* Epiphany
25 March *Ikostipémpti Martíou (tou Evangelismoú)* Greek Independence Day
1 May *Protomayiá* May Day
15 August *Dekapendávgoustos* (tis Panagías) Dormition Day
28 October *Ikostiogdóïs Oktovríou Óhi* ('No') Day, celebrating defiance of the 1940 Italian ultimatum
25 December *Hristoúgenna* Christmas Day
26 December *Sýnaxi Theotókou* Meeting of Virgin's Entourage
Moveable dates:
Kathará Dheftéra 1st day of Lent: 'Clean Monday'
Megáli Paraskeví Good Friday
Páskha Easter Sunday
tou Agíou Pnévmatos Whit (Pentecost) Sunday and Monday ('Holy Spirit'), end May or early-to-mid-June
Note: These moveable holidays are celebrated according to dates in the Greek Orthodox calendar, which usually differ from Catholic or Protestant dates.

R

RELIGION

The national religion of Greece is Greek Orthodoxy. You must dress modestly to visit churches and monasteries, which normally means long trousers for men, a long skirt or trousers for women and covered shoulders for both. However, men are often allowed to wear long shorts (over the knees) and skirts or wraps may be provided at the back of churches for women to cover themselves.

In Zákynthos Town, the church of Ágios Márkos on the eponymous plaza is Catholic, open during summer for the spiritual needs of visitors.

S

SMOKING

Since 2010, it has been illegal to smoke in any indoor space in Greece, including tavernas and bars. For a nation of inveterate puffers (though use is down in recent decades), compliance with the law is surprisingly good. But it is still allowed on unenclosed terraces or patios, thus such spaces are in high demand, even during cooler seasons. When you see ashtrays set out, you can be sure that the owner will not chivvy you for indulging. Vaping is big in Greece, and subject to the same strictures.

T

TELEPHONES

Local calling. There are no longer any area codes as such in Greece; even within the same local-call zone you must dial all 10 digits of the land-line number. What were the old codes are now merely the locators: 26950 or 26951 for all of Zákynthos. All Greek mobiles start with '69' and also total ten digits.

From overseas. To call Greece from abroad, first dial the international access code (00 from the UK), then 30 (the country code for Greece) and finally all 10 digits of the local number, be it land or mobile/cell.

Long distance from Greece. International direct dialling is available at very rare, noisy street-corner phone booths. These take phonecards (*tilekártes*), which are quite good value, as well as credit/debit cards. Pre-paid VoIP calling cards with a freephone access code and scratch-off PIN number are more common; they can be used from any phone and are by far the cheapest way to call abroad. To reverse charges (collect calls), dial 151 for Europe and 161 for the rest of the world. Overseas directory assistance is through the international operator (dial 161). For the local operator, dial 132. If your home mobile plan allows free or cheap roaming while in Greece, that is really the simplest, least expensive method of calling abroad while there.

Reverse-charge (collect) call **plirotéo apó to paralípti**

TIME ZONES

Greek time is GMT plus two hours. Daylight saving, when Greek clocks are put forward one hour, is observed from early on the last Sunday of March to early on the last Sunday of October. The chart shows the times in Greece and various other places during the European summer.

Los Angeles	New York	London	Paris	**Greece**	Sydney
2am	5am	10am	11am	**noon**	8pm

TIPPING

Greeks aren't obsessed with tipping, but it is the norm to leave a little more if service has been good, or the *kérazma* was particularly sumptuous. Usual amounts are as follows: hotel porter, €1 per bag; hotel room cleaner, €1 per day; waiter, 5–10 percent; taxi driver, just round up the meter amount; hairdresser/barber, 10 percent; lavatory attendant, €0.40–0.50.

TOILETS

Public conveniences are rare and best avoided. A better option is to use facilities at museums or the better cafés. If you do drop in specifically to use the toilet, it's customary to purchase coffee or some other drink before leaving.

Important note: you are always expected to put toilet tissue in the waste bin rather than down the toilet. Due to their narrow-bore pipes, toilets easily become clogged, and in rural areas it all goes to a soak pit which can't digest paper.

> Where is the toilet? **Pou íne i toualétta?**
> There's no paper! **Dhen ehei hárti toualéttas!**

TOURIST INFORMATION

The national Visit Greece entity (www.visitgreece.gr; still sometimes known as the GNTO or EOT in Greek) has the following offices abroad:

UK and Ireland: 5th Floor East, Great Portland House, 4 Great Portland Street, London W1W 8QJ; tel: (020) 7495 9300.

US and Canada: 800 Third Avenue, 23rd Floor, New York, NY 10022; tel: (212) 421 5777.

These offices supply general information and glossy pictures, but when it comes to anything specific on Zákynthos they are usually of little help. Zákynthos does not have an official tourism office.

TRANSPORT

Buses (*leoforía*). The public bus service on Zákynthos is patchy but, where it does exist, is very good value. Timetables are displayed at bus stops (ΣΤΑΣΕΙΣ – *stásis*) and at the KTEL bus station in Zákynthos Town (tel: 26950 22255/42656, www.ktel-zakynthos.gr), inconveniently located well southwest of the centre at Iatroú Mothonéou 2. Most services run between Zákynthos Town and Laganás Bay and Vasilikós. For all buses, buy your tickets on board or from nearby kiosks. You can flag a bus down or disembark anywhere within reason, though ideally at a signed stop.

Taxis. These are an expensive way to get around but may be your only option in parts of Zákynthos. Make sure the meter is switched on; there are two rates depending on time of day and whether you are inside or outside town. Large luggage in the boot attracts a surcharge of about €0.40 per item. Radio taxis can be summoned, for which there's also as small surcharge. Zante Taxi is one of the biggest companies (tel: 26950 48400, www.zantetaxi.gr).

Ferries. Frequent ferries run between Kyllíni on the mainland and Zákynthos Town. There is also a regular seasonal ferry from Ágios Nikólaos (Skinári), in the north of Zákynthos, to the tiny port of Pesádha on Kefaloniá. Itháki. For current ferry schedules and fares check with your nearest travel agent, the port authority (see under Emergencies) or online at www.goferry.gr.

What's the fare to…? **Póso éhi éna isitírio giá…?**
When's the next bus to…? **Póte févgi to epómeno leoforío yiá…?**

V

VISAS AND ENTRY REQUIREMENTS

All EU citizens may enter Greece to visit or work for an unlimited length of time. Citizens of Ireland can enter with a valid identity card or passport. British citizens must be in possession of a valid passport, which will be stamped upon entry and exit. As post-Brexit tourists, Brits are subject to Schengen Zone rules for length of stay – 90 days cumulative in any 180-day period. Fines for overstaying are horrendous, and any excuses short of documented confinement in hospital will not be entertained by officialdom.

Citizens of the US, Canada, Australia and New Zealand can stay for up to three months on production of a valid passport, with no advance visa required. South African citizens require a Schengen Visa, obtained in advance from a Greek embassy or full consulate. If you wish to extend these timescales you must obtain a permit from the proper department of the Zákynthos Town police station.

Greece has strict regulations about importing drugs. All the obvious ones are illegal, and there are strong punitive measures for anyone breaking the rules. Codeine and some tranquillisers are also banned. If you take any drug on the advice of your doctor, carry enough for your needs in an official container, as medicines for personal use are permitted.

Since the abolition of duty-free allowances for all EU countries, all goods brought into Greece from Britain must be duty-paid unless they are for personal use, not resale. In theory there are no limitations to the amount of duty-paid goods that can be brought into the country. However, cigarettes and most spirits are much cheaper in Greece than in Britain and Ireland (government duty is much lower, so waiting until you reach your destination to buy these goods will save you money).

For citizens of non-EU countries, allowances for duty-free goods brought into Greece are: 200 cigarettes or 50 cigars or 250g of tobacco; 1 litre of spirits or 4 litres of wine; 250ml of cologne or 50ml of perfume.

Non-EU residents can claim back Value Added Tax (currently between 6 and 24 percent) on any items costing over €120, provided they export the item within 90 days of purchase. Tax-rebate forms are available only at certain tourist shops and in-town merchants. Keep the receipt plus form and make your claim at the customs area of your departure airport.

Currency restrictions. There are no limits on the amount of euros visitors can import or export. There are no restrictions on travellers' cheques, but cash sums of more than $10,000/€10,000 or equivalent should be declared upon entry.

Covid-19 protocols. At present, Greece has suspended its prior requirement for inbound travellers to present evidence of having had at least three recognised covid inoculations, or a negative rapid antigen test result no older than two days before arrival date, or a negative PCR test result no older than three days before arrival. However, should there be a major resurgence of the disease, expect these or similar rules to be re-introduced; it would still be prudent to still travel with such documentation with you and it's always worth checking before you fly. Additionally, arrivals may again need to fill out an online Greek government Passenger Locator Form a day or two before travel, at https://travel.gov.gr/#/.

W

WEBSITES AND INTERNET ACCESS

Wi-Fi and internet cafés. As Wi-Fi is now available at just about all accommodation (sometimes charged for at fancier hotels) and almost all cafés/bars/restaurants. Very few internet cafés remain and only in Zákynthos Town; you are much better off with your phone or a tablet device within a wi-fi zone.

What's the code for your wi-fi? **Pió íne o kodikós yia to wi-fi?**

Websites. There are a number of useful websites for people travelling to Zákynthos:

www.visitgreece.gr/islands/ionian-islands/zakynthos The official Zákynthos page of the GNTO/EOT.

www.goferry.gr An excellent site giving online timetables for most Greek ferry routes.

https://zakynthosinformer.com Not just tourism info (including ferry schedules to/from Kefaloniá) but also local political and developmental gossip.

www.zanteweb.gr Comprehensive site with a wealth of information on Zákynthos, though be aware this is a commercial venture geared to steering you towards accommodation, excursion purveyors and car/taxi hire.

www.zanteisland.com Excellent site with information on Zákynthos, but as with the preceding one, a strong commercial aspect, with tie-ins to accommodation establishments.

WHERE TO STAY

Hotels are rated from 2-star to 5-star, an assessment based more on their common areas and amenities than the actual rooms (1-stars are effectively extinct and are anyway not found on Zákynthos). Rating establishes minimum price rates but prices can often vary widely within each class according to the season, location and availability of rooms, while ultra-luxury (5-star) establishments are not price controlled. Thus, a 3-star hotel room may be just as comfortable as a 5-star room, but common areas will not include a conference room, hairdresser, gym, spa or multiple restaurants. By law, current rates must always be posted in all rooms, usually on the main door or inside the closet; in practice this requirement is often ignored.

All hotels of 3-star rating and above are reasonably furnished, have en-suite rooms and should provide breakfast; rates below, unless specified otherwise, are quoted on a B&B basis. Breakfast is typically buffet, with a mix of fruit, juice, cereals, bread and/or cake, cold and warm dishes, plus often a 'live cooking' point where you can order pancakes, waffles or an omelette.

In high summer some form of air conditioning will enable you to get a good night's sleep. If your room doesn't have air conditioning (and a bare handful of the oldest properties still don't), there will either be a ceiling fan or you might be able to obtain a floor-standing fan from reception or the owner.

The majority of hotels listed here can be found on generic third-party booking sites, but many have their own websites which offer substantial discounts for direct booking. Although finding a room at short notice or on spec is not a problem for much of the year, it is still wise to reserve well in advance for the peak season of late July through the end of August. To telephone a hotel, dial the international country code for Greece (30), followed by the 10-digit number provided in our listings.

The price categories below are for a double room or studio with bath per night in high season, excluding August super peak periods. All hotel unit rates include VAT (Value Added Tax) of 13 percent. Most hotels in beach resorts are only open from April or May through October, and quite often even less than this – think June to September. Those in Zákynthos Town are open all year round.

€€€€€	above €300
€€€	€151–300
€€	€80–150
€	below €80

ZÁKYNTHOS TOWN

Hotel Alba €€ *Lámbrou Zivá 8, Zákynthos Town, tel: 26950 26641,* https://albahotel.gr. This small (just 13 units) three-star hotel is located in a fairly quiet area just two blocks in from the seafront. Facilities include air conditioning, small fridges and flat-screen TVs in the rooms, choice of bathtub or shower in the bathrooms, free wi-fi signal and room service.

Dali Luxury Rooms €€ *Lomvárdhou 20, tel: 26950 26016,* https://dalihotel.gr. One of the few *enikiazómena dhomátia* (rented rooms) establishments in the town, though with hotel accoutrements, these ten units (more basic ones with inland view, the others – including a few suites – with harbour view and small kitchenettes) live up to their 'luxury' tag with designer bathrooms and plush furnishings. It's a three-storey waterfront building, so the lift/elevator may well come in handy. Exceptionally helpful staff another bonus.

Hotel Palatino €€ *Kolokotróni 10 crnr Kolivá, Zákynthos Town, tel: 26950 27780,* https://palatinohotel.gr. A surprisingly good-value upmarket place. The rooms (including two junior suites and four family units), designed primariy for business travellers, have all mod cons, and the hotel as a whole is well tended and professionally run. Generous buffet breakfast provided; also a bar/lounge and restaurant for later in the day or night.

Hotel Plaza €€ *Kolokotróni 2, Zákynthos Town, tel: 26950 45733,* www.plazazante.gr. Probably the best-value hotel in town, in quiet Agía Triádha district, a short distance in from the town beach. Some of the units – which include suites and family rooms – have sea-view balconies. Lobby bar but no food service other than the expected breakfast buffet, which is rather good for the price.

Hotel Strada Marina €€ *Lomvárdou 14, Zákynthos Town, tel: 26950 42761,* www.stradamarina.gr. The largest place in Zákynthos Town, with 112 comfortable but not overly exciting rooms and suites, including family quads. In a vast modern building on the seafront, so many of the rooms have great views of the harbour. Breakfast buffet included, and there is a rooftop garden bar (June–Sept only) with a small pool.

VASILIKÓS AND LAGANÁS BAY

Crystal Beach €€€ *Kalamáki, tel: 26950 42774,* www.crystalbeach.gr. Large resort hotel, with rooms and suites in six categories for both package patrons and independent guests. Other facilities include a large sundeck- pool (despite the beach being literally just beyond the fence) with adjacent snack bar, plus the à la carte Pelouzo full-service sea-view restaurant. Oddly for such a rich pickings, there is no spa or gym.

Dimaras Apartments € *Porto Roma, Vasilikós, tel: 26950 35456 or 6985 976536,* https://dimarasapartments.gr. Simple but well-appointed doubles, studios and larger apartments (the latter either 'rustic' or 'premium' grade) are distributed over two buildings, in pretty and well-maintained gardens. This is set back from the beach, the rooms are very quiet, and the immediate surroundings are lovely and peaceful.

Fanero Guest House Kerí € *Inland, village centre, tel: 6978 195 264,* https:// fanero.gr. Just two 2022-built, state-of-the-art apartments here, one accommodating four persons, the other only two. Run by a branch of the same friendly family keeping Pansion Limni (see page 123). Each has a balcony and small kitchen.

Levantino Studios & Apartments € *Kamínia beach, On Vasilikós peninsula but just 8km from Town, tel: 26950 35366 or 6944 35 40 64,* https://levantino. gr. Two complexes here, dubbed I and II – I comprising studios and a stone house that can fit six and a sea view, while II, with more studios and larger apartments, is close to the sea at the town end of the Vasilikós Peninsula. All are equipped with a kitchen, and some look out over the gardens and sea, where the beach sports free-for-guests sunbeds and umbrellas. Good discounts available out of high season –up to half price.

Hotel Matilda €€ *Near Xirokástello village, Vasilikós peninsula, tel: 26950 35376,* www.matildahotel.gr. A designer, 4-star hotel on a hilltop, with commanding sea views from most of its five grades of rooms (including family units) and a large pool terrace. The grounds include a 40-acres of olive groves and fruit-tree orchards with walking paths through them. Operates only June to early Oct.

Pansion Limni € *Límni Kerioú beach, tel: 26950 48716,* www.pansionlimni. com. Welcoming and superb value pension just behind the far end of the beach. There are some larger, newer apartments at co-managed *Porto Tsi Ostrias* just 130m inland. Guests often receive gifts of home-made olive oil and wine. Minimum stay at either establishment is 4 nights.

Porto Koukla Beach Hotel €€€ *Lithakiá, tel: 26950 52393,* www.porto-koukla.com. This large hotel is situated at the western end of Laganás Bay. Popular mainly with German and Austrian visitors, Porto Koukla is well away from the tawdriness further east. Units consist of fair-sized doubles, triples and family rooms, many gazing out to Marathonisi (aka 'Turtle Island') in the bay. The hotel gardens back onto a narrow beach, which is overlooked by the hotel's excellent and inexpensive taverna (lunch noon–5pm, dinner buffet 7.30–9.30pm).

Sirocco Hotel €€ *Kalamáki, tel: 26950 26083,* www.siroccohotel.com. This is a good and reasonably quiet option in Kalamáki; the hotel's stylish standard rooms are a bargain out of season (or plump for equally stylish junior suites). There is a large swimming pool set in an attractive garden, and the beach is not too far away.

Vasilikos Beach €€€ *Ágios Nikólaos cove, tel: 26950 35325,* www.hotelvasilikosbeach.gr. Large hotel with airy rooms and suites in four categories feauring all mod cons, a large pool and a decent restaurant. The management also runs a popular water sports outfitter on the beach.

THE NORTH

Alexandra Beach Resort & Spa €€ *Tsiliví, tel: 26950 26190,* www.alexandrabeachresort.com. Located right on the beach in Tsiliví, this hotel offers on-site restaurant and bar as well as spa, gym and infinity pool. The spa features a sauna, jacuzzi as well as various therapies and treatments, including an on-site hairdressers. The plush rooms are ultra-comfortable with big comfy beds and just about everything you'd need for a relaxing stay. Some rooms offer pool views, while others offer sea views.

Al Mare Hotel € *Tsiliví, tel: 26950 25751,* www.almarehotel.gr. Perfectly located beach hotel around a 10-minute walk from Tsiliví centre. With heated outdoor pool, pool bar, cocktail lounge, restaurant and a separate pool for children. Rooms are clean and modern and come with balconies and garden views or sea views. There are plenty of sunbeds for use on the beach for hotel guests.

Amoudi Hotel € *Amoúdi, tel: 26950 62560,* www.amoudihotel.com. Tucked just inland from one of the nicer coves, between the busier resorts of Tsiliví and Alykés, this modern apart-hotel offers 1990s-decor units, from double and triple studios up to family apartments for 4, and there is a fine pool plus a well-regarded on-site restaurant, Kritamo, with Sunday 'Greek nights', to avoid or gravitate towards per taste.

Anemomilos (The Windmills) €€ *Korithí, Cape Skinári, tel: 26950 31132/31241,* www.zakynthoshotels.eu/Anemomilos-4468717. One of the most attractive places to stay on Zákynthos consists of two converted windmills and some cheaper stone-clad apartments at the very north end of the island. The managing Potamitis family also run the excellent nearby *To Faros* taverna as well as affordable trips to the nearby Blue Caves.

Anetis Beach Hotel € *Tsiliví, tel: 26950 28899,* www.anetishotel.gr. Compact (just 12 rooms, standard or superior) but pleasant place, set just back from the main beach (affiliated bar and sunbeds) in a lively but not abrasively noisy part of the resort. Superior rooms have designer bathrooms and sea-view balconies, though some standards also face the water. Be sure to ask ahead if it's a sea-view you're after.

Hotel La Caretta € *Alikanás, tel: 69964 86379,* www.zakynthoslacaretta.com. Great value, family-run hotel 8 minutes from the beach with a good on-site restaurant and pool.

Ionian Star Hotel €€ *Alykés, tel: 26950 83416,* www.ionian-star.gr. A smallish and very well-kept hotel, located just behind the beach. Spotless rooms and family apartments are excellent value, a spacious pool area beckons (plus there is a good on-site restaurant which specialises in Greek food). Open May–Oct.

Nobelos Seaside Lodge €€€€ *Ágios Nikólaos (Skinári), tel: 26950 31400,* www.nobelos.gr. This luxury spot in the north of the island is expensive but lovely. The four tastefully decorated suites occupy a traditional stone-built house on the south side of the bay here, each with individual character. Along with excellent service, breakfast is provided, a full-service 'bio' restaurant opens on site later in the day and there's a secluded nearby bay for swimming.

Panorama Apartments € *Ágios Nikólaos (Skinári), tel: 26950 31013,* www.zakynthoshotels.eu/Panorama_Apartments-1171589. A relatively modest but friendly establishment in its own grounds on a bluff just south of the village with cosy units, many affording sea views. Great value with simple breakfast included.

Plessas Palace €€ *Alikanás, near the village centre, almost a kilometre from the beach.* tel: 26950 41480, www.plessaspalace.com. The spacious rooms and studios in four categories, spread over three separate buildings, are decorated in warm colours, while other facilities include a pool, mini market and even a library. Advantageous half-board rates also offered.

Zante Palace €€ *Tsiliví, tel: 26950 49090,* www.zantepalace.com. This huge modern hotel is on Akrotíri bluff overlooking Tsiliví Bay, giving great views across to Kefaloniá. For what's on offer the standard doubles, double studios and larger apartments (which all enjoy bay views) are good value, and there is a nicely situated if somewhat small pool.

Zarkadis Apartments € *Tsiliví, tel: 26950 42786,* https://zarkadis.gr. Very comfortable, well-appointed apartments of varying sizes in an attractive building set in spacious leafy grounds (including a children's playground) just behind the beach, where sunbeds and umbrellas are provided gratis for guests.

INDEX

THE **MINI** ROUGH GUIDE TO
ZÁKYNTHOS

First edition 2023

Project editor: Annie Warren
Author: Marc Dubin
Picture Editor: Tom Smyth
Cartography Update: Carte
Layout: Katie Bennett
Head of DTP and Pre-Press: Katie Bennett
Head of Publishing: Kate Drynan
Photography Credits: Adobe Stock 4MC, 11, 40, 52, 55, 65; Dreamstime 20; iStock 16, 38, 77; Kevin Cummins/Apa Publications 67; Ministry of Culture and Sports 4TL; Mockford & Bonnetti/Apa Publications 31; Shutterstock 1, 4TC, 4MC, 4TC, 4ML, 4ML, 5T, 5M, 5M, 6T, 6B, 7T, 7B, 13, 19, 23, 26, 28, 32, 34, 36, 42, 44/45, 46, 47, 48, 51, 57, 58, 61, 62, 68, 71, 74, 76, 78, 80, 85
Cover Credits: The blue caves **Andrey Grinyov/Shutterstock**

Distribution

UK, Ireland and Europe: Apa Publications (UK) Ltd; sales@roughguides.com
United States and Canada: Ingram Publisher Services; ips@ingramcontent.com
Australia and New Zealand: Booktopia; retailer@booktopia.com.au
Worldwide: Apa Publications (UK) Ltd; sales@roughguides.com

Special Sales, Content Licensing and CoPublishing

Rough Guides can be purchased in bulk quantities at discounted prices. We can create special editions, personalised jackets and corporate imprints tailored to your needs. sales@roughguides.com; http://roughguides.com

Printed in China

This book was produced using **Typefi** automated publishing software.

Contact us

Every effort has been made to provide accurate information in this publication, but changes are inevitable. The publisher cannot be held responsible for any resulting loss, inconvenience or injury sustained by any traveller as a result of information or advice contained in the guide. We would appreciate it if readers would call our attention to any errors or outdated information, or if you feel we've left something out. Please send your comments with the subject line "Rough Guide Mini Zákynthos Update" to mail@uk.roughguides.com.